PRAISE FOR JIM COBB

"Jim Cobb is perhaps the most well-respected author in the preparedness community."

> —Joe Alton, MD, coauthor of *The Survival Medicine Handbook*

"Jim Cobb is one of the most practical, no-nonsense preparedness authors around. You can always count on him to cut through the nonsense of unrealistic advice and boil it down to logical, down-to-earth steps that will work for anyone."

> —Daisy Luther, founder of TheOrganicPrepper.com

"Jim Cobb is the voice of reason and experience with all things survival. If he says something works then you know you›re getting solid, field-tested information from a respected leader in the survival industry who is constantly applying his skills and incorporating what he teaches into his daily life."

> —Tony Nester, author of *Knife-Only Survival*

"Jim Cobb is a master at what it takes to survive in the city or anywhere. He provides you with the basic skills and knowledge for handling challenging situations ethically, with the big picture in mind. Jim gives you the tools and the knowledge for finding your path of self-reliance, for surviving with a smile when others are panicking."

> —Christopher Nyerges, author of *How to Survive Anywhere*

"Jim Cobb has rapidly established himself as one of the leading authorities in the preparedness and survival field. He has shown time and time again that he knows his stuff and, most importantly, knows how to convey that knowledge to his readers."

> —Scott B. Williams, author of *Bug Out*, *The Pulse*, and *The Darkness After*

T0059883

"In the disaster-preparedness community, most people just talk the talk. Jim Cobb is one of the few who walks the walk!"
—Creek Stewart, author of *Build the Perfect Bug Out Bag*

"If…you're serious about prepping, you should seek out serious advice. That means seeking out the experts who have no particular political or religious dogma to sell, experts who are laser-focused on what works. Jim Cobb is one such expert."
—Mike Mullin, author of *Ashfall*, *Ashen Winter*, *Darla's Story*, and *Sunrise*

PRAISE FOR *PREPPER'S HOME DEFENSE*

"*Prepper's Home Defense* has earned a place on my bookshelf by giving me the information I needed to go home and put in place some security procedures and equipment that made my home more secure the day I read the book."
—Stephanie Dayle, American Preppers Network

"Jim does a great job in laying out the options and helping the reader wade through all of the available weapons choices. I especially liked his improvised 'hand spike' fashioned from a hubcap removal tool… If you like reading about prepping—especially defense—you will like this book. It's a great compilation of security strategies to help protect your 'fort' and 'family.'"
—Creek Stewart, author of *The Unofficial Hunger Games Wilderness Survival Guide*

"Two things I especially like about the book are that it is realistic and that I couldn't find any really bad advice… I feel Cobb tells readers what they should hear, which is a credit to him."
—Charlie Palmer, author of *The Prepper Next Door*

PRAISE FOR *THE PREPPER'S COMPLETE BOOK OF DISASTER READINESS*

"Unlike many of the books in this genre, Jim's does not resort to scare tactics—one of my pet peeves. I highly recommend this book. The information is well researched and just might save your life."

> —Arthur T. Bradley, PhD, author of *Prepper's Instruction Manual* and *Handbook to Practical Disaster Preparedness for the Family*

"Jim Cobb has been a 'go-to guy' on the internet for a long time, and I think with this volume, he's collected a canon of survival knowledge and training. The chapters on survivalism in fiction and the survival library section are worth it alone."

> —Sean T. Page, author of *The Official Zombie Handbook*, *War Against the Walking Dead*, and *Zombie Survival Manual*

PREPPER'S LONG-TERM SURVIVAL GUIDE

SECOND EDITION

FOOD, SHELTER, SECURITY, OFF-THE-GRID POWER,
AND MORE LIFESAVING STRATEGIES FOR
SELF-SUFFICIENT LIVING

JIM COBB

Published by:
Ulysses Press
PO Box 3440
Berkeley, CA 94703
www.ulyssespress.com

ISBN: 9-781-64604-444-3
Library of Congress Control Number: 2022944061

Printed in the United States by Sheridan Books Minnesota
10 9 8 7 6 5 4 3 2

Project editor: Renee Rutledge
Managing editor: Claire Chun
Proofreader: Ariel Adams
Indexer: S4Carlisle
Cover and interior design: what!design @ whatweb.com
Cover artwork: from shutterstock.com—person using water filter © Timothy Epp;
    canned goods © Cara Purdy; army knife © Volegzhanina Elena; aermotor windmill
    © Kenneth Keifer; matchstick © Joe Belanger; cartridges © svich
Layout: Winnie Liu

For Mom and Grandma—I hope I've made you both proud.

CONTENTS

INTRODUCTION

Nowadays you can't throw a dart while blindfolded in a bookstore without hitting a survival manual of some sort. From bug-out bags to food pantry organization, prepping topics fill the shelves. Click over to your favorite online bookseller and you'll find e-book after e-book extolling the virtues of having extra batteries for flashlights and making sure you have the latest and greatest water filtration system, just in case.

It wasn't always like that, though. Back when I was a kid, at the height of the Cold War, about the only survival books you could find were centered on wilderness skills. How to make a debris hut and get a fire going until you were rescued—that type of thing. While I devoured those books and had great fun "going native" in the woods near my home, it wasn't until a fateful purchase of my father's that I truly got the prepping bug.

I'd always been a voracious reader, even as a young child. Science fiction, horror, and action/adventure were my genres of choice. One day, my dad was at the mall and stopped in a B. Dalton bookstore. A display of paperbacks caught his eye, and he thought I might be interested in reading at least the first book in a new series called *The Survivalist* by Jerry Ahern. Within mere minutes after he handed it to me, I started in on it and was immediately riveted. Nuclear missiles raining down on America! Gunfights with nasty bikers! And, oh man, what was the deal with the secret retreat hidden inside a freakin' mountain?

Not long after that, I happened to stumble across a copy of *Life After Doomsday* by Bruce D. Clayton. Here was the perfect complement to the fiction I'd been reading. It gave detailed instructions on how to be prepared to survive a nuclear war, just like John Thomas Rourke in Ahern's novels. This book truly sealed my fate, as it were, to become what we call today a "prepper."

I studied, and then put my studies to use. I built an obscene number of survival kits of various shapes, sizes, and configurations. I learned how to shoot, how to purify water, and how to stockpile food and supplies.

Flash forward a couple decades, and now prepping has become rather mainstream. As that happened, naturally all sorts of writers jumped on the proverbial bandwagon. Many of these books were and still are excellent references, such as *Build the Perfect Survival Kit* by John D. McCann and *The Unofficial Hunger Games Wilderness Survival Guide* by Creek Stewart. But quite a few other books have been, shall we say, less than ideal.

Time and again, the books and manuals tell readers exactly what to do until power is restored, until help arrives in some form, or until they find their way back to civilization after being lost. They spell out lists and lists of bug-out bag contents, eighty-five different ways to build a fire, and how to set a broken leg with paracord and a stick.

But what if the lights *never* come back on? What if there is no help coming...*ever*? This long-term scenario is something that has always been lacking in survival nonfiction.

Until now.

What you hold in your hands is the key to surviving weeks, months, even years after the initial disaster. We'll go well beyond bugging out and instead focus on becoming self-sufficient in the wake of a major calamity. Of course, much of the information here is just as applicable today, while times are whatever passes for normal, as they are after an electromagnetic pulse (EMP) takes out the grid from coast to coast.

If you are forward thinking enough to realize a stockpile of food to last even a solid month may not be enough to last the duration of a pandemic, keep reading.

If you are truly concerned about how you would keep your family alive and safe after society has collapsed around your ears, this book is just what you're seeking.

If you are willing to make serious preparations to withstand the long-term effects of the New Madrid fault slipping in a major way or the Yellowstone Caldera finally blowing its top, you have come to the right place.

Let's go for a walk to the far end of the preparedness trail. We're going to skip past the blizzards, the wind storms, and the stranded-in-the-woods scenarios and get right into the heart of long-term survival planning. Don't worry, I'll be right beside you. I'll do my best to make sure you don't get lost along the way.

AUTHOR'S NOTE

To help illustrate what life may truly be like in the wake of a major disaster, each of the following chapters is prefaced by a fictional entry from a journal or diary, ostensibly written during the weeks that follow an EMP strike in the United States.

CHAPTER 1

LONG-TERM EVENTS: LEARNING FROM HISTORY TO PREVENT FUTURE DÉJÀ VU

It has been 112 days since the lights went out and didn't come back on. I know this because the last thing I do every night, after checking all the locks one more time, is cross off the day on the calendar. Four months ago, had anyone told me a major disaster was right around the corner, I'd have snorted at them for being "doom and gloom."

I've been meaning to start this journal for months now. I kept putting it off because there is always so much to do, and by sundown I'm ready to just collapse into bed. But, while I make no promises to update this thing every day, I do want there to be some sort of record, some documentation, of what we've endured so far and will continue to experience as the days progress. Heh, who knows? Maybe decades from now, if the country ever gets back on its feet, they'll talk about this journal in schools across the land.

Four months ago, I could take a hot shower three times a day if I wanted. Today, I bathe once a week at most, in tepid water that three others have already used.

Sixteen weeks ago, I had my choice of any number of restaurants for dinner. Today, we eat whatever we can find, grow, hunt, or trap.

One hundred and twelve days ago, I was living the American Dream. Today, I'm living a nightmare.

Welcome to the end of the world.

When we talk about long-term events, we are referring to catastrophes that effectively bring society to a screeching halt, along with all the associated chaos and confusion one would expect. Tornadoes and hurricanes, while certainly disastrous in their own rights, don't bring with them quite the level of societal collapse we're looking at here.

Thankfully, these events don't happen very often, but when they do, it takes a long time to return to some semblance of normalcy. To better illustrate the point, let's start by taking a look at some historical examples.

PANDEMICS

Well, there's a word that pretty much everyone is tired of hearing. I'm writing this in the spring of 2022. We've been dealing with COVID-19 globally for a little over two full years. One thing that many people were very slow to realize was that even if you don't believe in the severity of a situation, you're still going to be affected by the reactions to it.

Early on, as officials at all levels of the government started shutting things down in the interest of safety, people shopped like locusts, wiping shelves clean of just about everything. The Great Toilet Paper Panic of 2020 went into full swing. When the TP ran out, they bought bath wipes, paper towels, facial tissues, and anything else that might be a workable substitute.

On one hand, as far as disaster scenarios go, we've had it pretty good. For most of the United States, Netflix has been readily available, as has Amazon, Walmart, and take-out food. Nobody has been dressing up in ragged biker/fetish outfits, at least not out of necessity. Who knew that the official dress code of the apocalypse would be pajamas and bed head?

On the other hand, though, people have been angry. Well, that's an understatement. Many spent the heart of the pandemic absolutely livid pretty much all day, every day, rivaling Yosemite Sam in his worst rootin' tootin', full-on apoplectic rage. They weren't just throwing punches over a pack of Cottonelle but were about as nasty as they could be on social media. While the internet has never been known for polite and civil discourse, it got absolutely brutal in short order. People who were generally easy going and affable came up with ever-more creative ways to tell people to go off and commit physically impossible acts with themselves…for daring to argue about the weather.

Two years into the pandemic, not a whole lot has changed. The shortages at stores are still happening, for a variety of reasons that range from staffing issues to a decline in raw material production. And people are still angry, though it is more of a long simmer than a ranging inferno.

By all accounts, it is likely to get worse before it gets better, so there's that to look forward to as well.

FAMINE

Famine is defined as a widespread lack of food, causing a sharp increase in fatalities on a regional level. Basically, something causes crop failure or in some other way limits the amount of available food in a given area over a period of time. For example, a long-term drought could result in a significant lack of food crops being available. Famine could also result from political upheavals, as when an oppressive government negatively affects food distribution.

Occasionally, both natural and political factors can combine, causing something akin to a perfect storm of food shortages. In July 1995, a series of massive floods occurred in North Korea. The floodwaters utterly destroyed crops, arable land, and, perhaps most importantly, emergency grain reserves. Given the already tumultuous political climate and declining economy, North Korea didn't have the capability to bring in resources from outside the country.

While precise figures may never be known due to the lack of reliable information coming out of North Korea even today, estimates range up to three million deaths directly attributable to the famine.

One of the most well-known famines is the Irish Potato Famine. From 1845 to 1852, approximately one million people died in Ireland as a result of a potato blight that wiped out the primary source of food. Another million or so people managed to flee the country. Between the famine deaths and the mass exodus, the overall population of Ireland dipped by about 20 to 25 percent during this period.

At the time, roughly 30 percent of the population were entirely dependent upon the potato for food. Further, most of them relied on a single variety of potato, called the Irish Lumper. Because of the lack of genetic diversity among the crops, the blight was particularly devastating.

It wasn't just starvation that killed people during the Irish Potato Famine, nor in any other famine. As people starve, their immune systems begin to falter. This, coupled with the gradual lack of services providing medical care, clean water, and other necessities, causes significant outbreaks of disease.

We may live in a nation of plenty right now, but what if the ever-changing climate were to take a turn for the worst and cause massive crop failures? The domino effect from even one or two bad seasons could send the country into a tailspin.

ECONOMIC COLLAPSE

Of the various types of long-term disasters, perhaps the most difficult to define is economic collapse. Many situations would fall under this umbrella, such as hyperinflation or a lengthy economic depression resulting in mass bankruptcies and high unemployment. No matter the cause, one thing almost all economic collapses have in common is mass civil unrest.

In 1998, Russia experienced an economic collapse that resulted in bank closures and mass runs on basic commodities. Inflation rose to about

84 percent. By comparison, the United States currently averages around 1.6 percent inflation. Prices for food went up almost 100 percent, while at the same time the ruble decreased in value. Millions of people saw their entire life savings disappear as banks failed.

Those Russians living in urban areas were the worst off. With no homegrown crops to sustain them, they were forced to stand in long lines for the most meager of supplies. The elderly living on pensions suddenly found the much-needed money completely cut off. Hospitals were also affected, seeing massive reductions in already scarce drug supplies.

While the Russian economy did rebound rather quickly due to rising oil prices the following year, I don't think they are out of the woods completely, even today.

Around this same time, Argentina experienced its own collapse. After several years of economic instability, including at least two bouts of hyperinflation, the bottom finally fell out in 2001. By the end of that year, unemployment had risen to about 20 percent. As a result of people pulling their pesos from the bank, converting them to dollars, and then sending them abroad, the government froze bank accounts for twelve months, allowing only very small withdrawals each week. This measure naturally did not go over very well, and people took to the streets to protest. While many of these demonstrations started out peacefully enough, albeit loud, they were soon accompanied by property damage and violence. It took several years before anything that could be called recovery began to take place.

What would you do if the government suddenly froze your bank account? What if what little money you could scrounge was all but worthless?

FREAK OCCURRENCES

Things like economic collapse and pandemics don't typically happen overnight. There is usually a chain of events, though perhaps imperceptible at the time, that takes us from Point A to Point B and on down the line. However, history has also witnessed events that occurred so suddenly and had such long-ranging effects, it is almost mind-boggling.

In 1815, volcanic Mount Tambora, located on the Indonesian island of Sumbawa, violently erupted. This remains the single largest volcanic eruption in recorded history. The eruption column rose about twenty-eight miles, spewing over sixty cubic miles of dust and debris. The ash that jetted into the atmosphere created something akin to a nuclear winter. Temperatures across the globe fell for a year or more.

The so-called "Year Without a Summer" was the result of those falling temps. The abnormal cold wiped out many crops. In June 1816, frosts were being reported in New York. Lake ice was seen in Pennsylvania in July and August. In some areas, only 10 percent of the crops planted were eventually harvested. This drove the price of grains up, tripling in some places.

HORROR STORIES

Believe it or not, the Tambora eruption helped create two of the most popular horror icons in modern history. A group of friends were vacationing in Switzerland that summer, and the poor weather forced them to stay inside for much of their trip. A contest was set up between the friends to see who could write the scariest story. Mary Shelley won the contest with her story Frankenstein, or the Modern Prometheus. A second member of the party, Lord Byron, wrote A Fragment, which later inspired a third member of the group, John William Polidori, to write The Vampyre. This work, in turn, greatly influenced Bram Stoker's Dracula.

On June 30, 1908, an explosion occurred in Siberia near the Podkamennaya Tunguska River. This explosion was about a thousand times more powerful than the atomic bomb dropped on Hiroshima. It is believed to have been either a meteoroid or a comet that exploded about five miles from the ground. The explosion leveled pretty much everything within almost eight hundred square miles.

Due to the remote location, it took several years for scientific investigators to mount an expedition to the site. What they found at ground zero was an area about five miles across containing upright trees that were scorched and missing all limbs. Moving outward from there, trees were completely flattened, all falling away from the site of the explosion. Because the explosion happened in the middle of nowhere, there were no known human casualties.

However, what if something like the Tunguska event were to happen today, say a few miles above New York City? Meteoroids enter Earth's atmosphere every day. Most of them burn up before hitting the ground, and those that survive the fall are usually rather small. But an explosion or strike in a populated area would have serious, lasting consequences.

¤ ¤ ¤ ¤

Now, keep in mind that this has been just a walk through a few highlights from the past. There are many other long-term events we didn't touch on, along with examples of entire cultures and societies that fell apart, such as the Romans and the Mayans.

What sorts of calamities might the future bring? What events will shape the world to come? Let's take a look at some of the more likely suspects.

NEW MADRID EARTHQUAKE

When you say the word "earthquake," most Americans think immediately of California. I mean, how often would thoughts turn to the Midwest?

The New Madrid fault runs along the southeastern edge of the Midwest. Extending roughly 150 miles in length, it goes from Illinois through Missouri, Arkansas, and Tennessee. Several thousand earthquakes have been reported in this area over the last four decades, with most of them being way too small to be felt by residents. However, that certainly wasn't the case in 1811–1812. Beginning with two quakes on December 16, 1811, this seismic zone went into an uproar. These quakes were powerful enough to be felt hundreds of miles away. They caused sidewalks in Washington, DC to crack and church bells to ring in Boston.

With so many tremors happening every year, this is obviously an area with a lot of seismic instability. Should the fault finally decide to give way, the damage and loss of life could be staggering. Some experts believe a major quake along the New Madrid fault is inevitable, perhaps within the next few decades.

Should that come to pass, it would make any of the California earthquakes look like a child's temper tantrum by comparison. Unlike those of the West Coast, the building codes in the New Madrid fault zone have given a nod to seismic safety only in the last twenty years or so. Anything built prior to that won't hold up in an earthquake.

If you thought the government responses to Hurricanes Katrina and Rita were ineffectual, can you imagine just how overstretched the emergency response would be to a disaster that encompasses several poorly prepared states?

YELLOWSTONE CALDERA

While this threat is becoming a little more recognized by the general public, many people still do not realize the home of the much-vaunted geyser Old Faithful rests atop a huge underground volcano. Imagine a vast underground bubble of magma or molten rock. If it gets emptied, say through an eruption, the land above that bubble may collapse. That's called a caldera.

The Yellowstone Caldera was formed 640,000 years ago after what is sometimes called a *supervolcano* erupted. While there weren't any scientists around back then to take notes, they've postulated that this eruption sent about 240 cubic miles of ash and debris into the air. Now, go back and reread what I said about the eruption of Mount Tambora and the effects it had on the world. The amount of debris sent flying then was about one-quarter of what the Yellowstone supervolcano managed.

If there were another comparable eruption at Yellowstone, and many scientists say we're entirely overdue for one, we're talking about a true end-of-life-as-we-know-it scenario. It would plunge the entire planet into a mini Ice Age. Solar radiation reaching the Earth's surface would be minimal. There simply wouldn't be a growing season at all in most regions, not in the immediate future. Ash would fall like snow for days, possibly weeks. The air quality would diminish greatly as well, due to all the soot and particulates floating around.

If you want to read what I feel is a pretty accurate portrayal of what life would be like after such an event, pick up a copy of *Ashfall* by Mike Mullin.

ELECTROMAGNETIC PULSE (EMP)

We've all experienced temporary power outages. A few hours, no big deal. A couple days, pain in the posterior but easily endured. But what if the lights *never* came back on?

Essentially, an EMP is a short burst of electromagnetic energy. It causes electrical current surges, which may damage a wide range of devices. While we typically use things like surge suppressors to protect our electronics from lightning strikes, they would be of little use for protection against a large EMP strike.

We face the risk of an EMP damaging the electrical grid in the United States in two different ways. First, it could occur as part of an enemy attack. EMP is a byproduct of nuclear detonation. Scientists found that out after the Starfish Prime atomic bomb test in 1962. A high-altitude nuclear explosion was set off 250 miles above a point in the middle of the Pacific Ocean. The resulting EMP took out streetlights in Hawaii, almost *900 miles away*. From that, we can extrapolate that if a similar device were detonated 250 miles above Indianapolis, Indiana, there would be loss of electrical power from Dallas, Texas, to New York City. And that's limiting it to 1960s nuclear technology.

Congressional studies seem to indicate that as few as two small nuclear devices detonated in the right places could take out 70 percent or more of our electrical capabilities. Several countries have this technological capability right now, and more will likely join the list soon. This is one of the reasons why we get a little uptight when nations like North Korea want so badly to have successful rocket launches.

The second way we could get hit with an EMP is through a geomagnetic storm sent via the sun. Back in 1859, we experienced what has been dubbed the Carrington Event. In September of that year, the Earth was bathed in a coronal mass ejection from the sun. You've heard of the aurora borealis, right? While that light show is usually confined to northern locations like Alaska or Norway, the Carrington Event was seen as far from the poles as Hawaii and Cuba. There were some negative aspects to those pretty lights, though. Telegraph systems were dramatically affected, in some places catching on fire. Back then, of course, those telegraphs represented the height of technology. This was way before electric devices became commonplace. It wasn't until the early 1900s that cities began installing electric lights, for example.

Care to place a bet on just how bad things could get if a similar solar storm happened today, or if some terrorist faction got their hands on an EMP device? Think about how dependent we are upon electricity nowadays. From the alarm clocks that wake us up, the TV that brings us the news and weather forecast, to the almighty smart phones that keep us connected to the world at large, all of that and more would be rendered useless in the blink of an eye. Heck, if Facebook goes down for an hour, some folks act like it's the end of the world.

The effect wouldn't be limited to conveniences like computers and alarm clocks. Pretty much anything that contains circuitry would be dead. While there is some debate as to the exact effect it would have on vehicles, it is fairly certain the power grid itself would be in shambles and likely remain so for quite some time.

Something that is often overlooked in discussions about EMP is the fact that while we have the know-how to build more transformers and such to replace any infrastructure that is damaged by EMP, those repairs don't happen overnight. It would take literally years before any semblance of life as we know it could be restored.

WAR AND TERRORISM

Leaving the politics out of the discussion, terrorist acts and outright declarations of war remain a constant risk. A couple of guys in Boston set off two bombs and managed to effectively shut down the entire city. That's exactly how terrorism works. It spreads fear, confusion, and chaos. In some ways, it is like watching a magician who is particularly talented with misdirection. Only instead of a dove appearing in one hand while you've been watching the other hand do card tricks, it is the sniper distracting you from seeing the car bomb.

Ever since 9/11, Americans have seen many of their rights slowly erode away in the name of security. Believe it or not, there was a time not too long ago when visiting the tax assessor's office at the county courthouse didn't require you to all but strip down to your skivvies just to get past security. Some believe we're not too far away from seeing martial law enacted in some areas, complete with soldiers at every street corner asking to see your papers.

Something that is rarely taught in public schools is what happened to Japanese Americans during World War II. On February 19, 1942, President Franklin D. Roosevelt signed Executive Order 9066, authorizing the military to remove all people of Japanese ancestry from the West Coast of the United States and place them into internment camps. It did not matter that many of these people were full-fledged American citizens. The US Census Bureau assisted in this program, opening its records to the military. As many as 110,000 to 120,000 people were detained in these camps.

This all happened as a reaction to the Japanese attack on Pearl Harbor. Our nation certainly has a habit of overreacting to situations, doesn't it?

Of course, we still face the possibility that another nation might openly attack us, using nuclear missiles, conventional weapons, or even the EMP devices discussed earlier. While we would, I have no doubt, prevail in such a conflict, we'd likely suffer at least some damage. Odds are pretty good too that the effects of such an attack would be long-standing. Generally speaking, weapons get more, not less, powerful as technology advances. If some foreign entity were to send a missile strike, and even one or two managed to sneak through our defenses, the damage and loss of life could be enormous.

¤ ¤ ¤ ¤

The point of this walk through both the past and potential future is to illustrate the very real risk of long-term disasters. As humans, we all have a tendency to become complacent. If we've not seen a major catastrophe in our lifetimes, we often feel as though one could never happen. Sure, we've had hurricanes and tornadoes, floods, and even a pretty bad terrorist attack right in the heart of New York City. But I doubt many of us have seen a total societal collapse, not up close and personal.

Does that mean you should fear what may be coming? Well, there's no simple answer to that question. Yes, there exists the distinct possibility that during your lifetime something may happen to turn the world, or at least *your* world, on its ear. That probably should scare you a little bit. But, right now at least, you have the luxury of being able to take steps, to make plans, so you'll be in a better position than you're in today should the worst come to pass.

CHAPTER 2

WATER: WATER EVERYWHERE AND NOT A DROP TO DRINK

A few years back, I was channel surfing one night and caught part of a movie that had something to do with talking lizards living in what looked like a town from the Old West. (Hey, I didn't write it.) There was a scene where it starts to rain and everyone in town rushes outside with every pot, pan, and bucket they can find to catch the rainwater. That's pretty much what it's like when it rains here now. Those of us who have rain gutters have buckets or barrels in place all the time. It's surprising how many homes in our neighborhood don't have any gutters at all! I'd never paid any attention to that before, but many of the homes that were built or extensively remodeled in the last several years don't have a single gutter run anywhere. Those folks are really hurting now.

Water is another of those things we always just took for granted. Turn on the faucet and, voilà, all the water you could ever want. On top of that, it seemed as though every person you met on the street was carrying a bottle of water. It's been a long time since we had the luxury of going to the store and choosing which brand of water we liked the most.

We manage to make do with what water we can harvest from the rain as well as rationing out our remaining bottles. Outside of standing in the rain collecting what we can, it has been quite some time since we were able to take actual showers. Thankfully, we have been managing about a bath a week or so. Well, "bath" might be an exaggeration. We have an old metal washtub that we used to use for giving the dogs baths. We save all the water we've been using for cleaning dishes and clothes, dumping it into the tub. After several days, we have about five or six inches of water in the tub. Haul the tub up above a fire pit to heat it up and then we take turns bathing. By the time the last person gets their turn, the water isn't all that warm anymore, but it beats just having another sponge bath. Once everyone has washed up, the water gets poured into the garden. Waste not, want not, and all that.

It is said that the human body can survive about three days without water. While that might be technically accurate, I sure wouldn't want to be a test case. We need to regularly consume water to even approach some degree of good health. We also use water for hygiene purposes, as well as for washing clothes and other items. If you sit down and do the math, adding up every gallon of water you use in just a single day, you'll likely be shocked. The average person uses somewhere in the neighborhood of one hundred gallons a day. Your own average might be a bit north or south of that, depending on personal habits. The good news, though, is that all the water you'll be using need not be potable. But, it's safe to say that you'll need far more than just a couple cases of bottled water if you're planning to survive an extended emergency.

There are basically four primary sources of water to consider: water you've stored, drilled wells, rainwater, and what we'll call "wild" sources such as rivers and lakes.

WATER STORAGE

Storing water involves a few issues that need to be planned for in advance. Water is what it is. By that, I mean it is heavy, it takes up a certain amount of space, and nothing can be done about either of those factors. It cannot be compressed into a smaller size, and it sure can't be made lighter. There is really no such thing as dehydrated water!

Because few people have unlimited space to use for water storage, you'll need to prioritize what truly needs to be done with the limited water you have.

Planning for consumption should always come first. We often think of dehydration as something that is relegated to times of hot weather and heavy exertion. While those factors do increase the risk of dehydration, the fact is many people are at least mildly dehydrated on a daily basis. Few of us really buckle down and drink as much water as our bodies need. That's going to be even more difficult to do when supplies are limited.

After consumption, the next priority is hygiene, such as frequent handwashing. Illness can spread quickly throughout a home and community when hygiene isn't kept up properly. Store-bought hand sanitizer is okay, but it won't last forever. Hands should be washed after every bathroom use as well as before prepping any food.

Anything you can do to keep at least somewhat clean, particularly washing hands regularly as well as taking good care of your teeth, will help reduce the instances of illness and infection. It is also important from a morale standpoint. Survivors will feel better about the situation if they can wash up and feel human.

Water used for hygiene need not be absolutely pure. The exception would be water used for brushing teeth, as it is almost impossible not to ingest at least a bit of it. You might want to run rainwater through a cloth filter to remove the dead bugs, but otherwise, it is good to go as far as bathing is concerned.

PROPERLY STORING TAP WATER

If you are on municipal water, there is likely already enough chlorine and other additives to it that it will store just fine for several months. However, whether that's the case or if instead you have a well, it isn't the worst idea to add a bit of bleach to the water prior to sealing the container. Fill the container almost all the way to the top, then add a few drops of non-scented chlorine bleach. Given that this is water that should be potable already, you only need to add a couple drops per gallon of water to prevent any nasties from multiplying. Fill the container the rest of the way, then swirl it around so a few drops of water splash out on to the threads where the cap screws on. This ensures no bacteria or other organisms are able to sneak in after putting the cap on the container.

One gallon of water weighs around eight pounds. While most people can easily handle moving a single gallon of water, it adds up quickly when you store it in bulk containers. For example, one product I use is the Aqua-Tainer jug. It holds seven gallons of water in a food-safe plastic container, complete with handle and nifty little foldout spigot. Full, it weighs about thirty-five pounds, which is probably a good upper limit for a portable container. Once you get much heavier than that, many people will have real difficulty moving it. I myself can easily lift it with one hand, but I sure wouldn't want to run a race with it!

Portability is something you need to keep in mind with water storage. If you want to set up fifty-five-gallon drums as rain barrels, that's a great idea, but recognize that once they're even two-thirds full, those barrels aren't going anywhere, at least not easily.

It is important, though, to have at least some amount of water set aside. Honestly, you can't store too much water. If it is stored properly, it isn't going to go bad, and, let's face it, water is something you'll always need to use, emergency situation or not. Even though properly stored water won't get rancid, I do suggest rotating your stored water about every six months. Use the old water for your garden or animals. Getting into the habit of rotating your water storage will help keep you assured of exactly how much you have on hand at any given time.

Start with buying several cases of bottled water. If you shop around and watch for sales, you can get some good deals and not cause too big a dent in your wallet. The point of having these cases of water is to give you a bridge, so to speak, between the first few days of the crisis and the time when you'll be totally dependent upon alternative sources. You know, beyond a shadow of a doubt, that the bottled water is safe, which can give you tremendous peace of mind while you set your other plans in motion. Plus, bottled water, even in cases, is very easy to move around. Stash it all in the basement or in the back of closets to reduce the temptation for family members to grab bottles here and there.

WHAT ABOUT SWIMMING POOLS?

Invariably, someone new to prepping sees that nice, big swimming pool in the backyard as a great way to store water. I mean, hey, it's already there, right? Here's the problem: To make sure the water stays nice and clean for swimming, we have to add chlorine to it. I know, I know, that's what municipal water departments do to our drinking water as well. The problem lies in the additional chemicals that are mixed with the chlorine used to treat swimming pools. These chemicals, called stabilizers, serve to keep the chlorine working longer before it finally gasses off. It is those chemicals that can be harmful to us if we consume pool water in any real quantities.

That doesn't mean that ten-thousand-gallon swimming pool is of no practical use. Far from it! Use that water for washing clothes, bathing, flushing toilets, that sort of stuff. Doing so frees up the potable water for drinking and cooking.

Keeping in mind that our focus here is on long-term survival scenarios, even the most ambitious prepper would be hard-pressed to store enough bottled water to last a family more than perhaps a few months at most. Using a family of four as an example, if each case amounts to about 3 gallons, they'll need to store about ten cases for each week of the crisis. Not too difficult to do to prep for a week or two, but 40 cases per month will take up some serious floor space.

Remember, too, that all of those numbers are based on an average consumption of 1 gallon of water per person, per day. That's just-barely subsistence levels of hydration in many cases. Sure, in the middle of winter when most of your time is spent indoors, 1 gallon might suffice. In the middle of summer, when everyone is working in the gardens and such, not so much. Regardless of climate and workload being performed, 1 gallon per day isn't going to allow for much of any bathing, not to mention laundry, pets, gardens, and other areas of life that need water.

Look at water storage as a stopgap measure. Meaning, the water you store in cases and bulk containers in the basement or under beds is for the short term, to get you over the hump while you implement more sustainable sorts of solutions. Store as much water as is feasible for your family, but recognize that you'll never be able to store enough for a long-term scenario. You'll eventually need to turn to other sources.

WELLS

Being on a private well, as opposed to municipal water, puts you a step ahead of the game...kind of. See, wells need pumps to bring the water up to your house. Well pumps work on electricity, of course. No juice, no water.

All hope is not lost, however. There are hand pumps that can be purchased and installed inside a home's well system. What is nice about these devices is that they can pressurize the water and allow you to use your faucets and taps just as you would today. The downside is the cost. Expect to pay in the neighborhood of $1,000 for one of these hand pump systems. They are not difficult to install and can be easily stored for future use.

RAINWATER CATCHMENT SYSTEMS

If you don't have gutters on your home or garage, I highly suggest you look into installing them yourself or having them installed by a professional. It isn't cheap, I know. Depending on your location and the size of your house, expect to pay upwards of a few thousand dollars when all is said and done. But, it is infinitely harder to collect rainwater in any quantity without the use of gutters. Think about it like this: If your roof is about a thousand square feet, just a half inch of rainfall will give you about three hundred gallons of water flowing through those gutters and into barrels.

Depending on the configuration of your house and outbuildings, the ideal would be having rain barrels set up at each gutter downspout. If that's not doable for some reason, do the best you can. Whether you have just one downspout that can work with a barrel or several, consider daisy-chaining multiple rain barrels together so that when the first one fills up, the runoff goes to the next in line. While this is a fairly simple DIY project, you can also buy readymade kits from several sources that will provide all the materials and instructions you need.

No matter how you set up the rain barrels, be sure to have an easy way to access the water inside. A built-in spigot near the bottom is probably the best and is far better than dunking in buckets. With the spigot, you can run a garden hose to wherever you want to use the water, such as in a garden bed. Also, make sure the barrels have tight-fitting lids to help prevent insects and debris from getting inside. You'll still have to filter the water before consuming it (more on that subject below) as it will have picked up bits of roofing and other detritus as it flowed down into the barrels, but anything you can to do keep more junk from getting into the water will be beneficial.

There are many different types of rain barrels readily available for purchase at just about any decent-sized hardware store. You can also sometimes pick up food-grade barrels fairly cheap from Craigslist or similar sources. These used barrels will need to be thoroughly cleaned. Personally, I prefer to purchase actual rain barrels from a trustworthy source, lest someone try to sell me a "food-grade" barrel that once contained some sort of toxic chemical.

One option you might consider is placing one or more barrels inside a garage or shed. This will serve to keep prying eyes from seeing them. Stop in at your local hardware store or garden shop and ask about gutter diverters. This is a device that is installed on a downspout to divert the water into a hose that runs into the rain barrel. Once the barrel is full, the diverter will allow the water to continue through the downspout and onto the ground. You can run the hose from the diverter through a small hole in the wall and into the rain barrel you've stashed inside. While most diverters blend in fairly well with the gutter system, you might hedge your bet by setting this up only on the back side of the garage or shed, where it won't be quite as visible. Be sure to caulk around the hole very well to prevent insect infestations.

Even if you don't plan to use this sort of hidden rainwater catchment system, those diverters are handy to have as they will keep water from overflowing out of the barrels and gushing onto your home's foundation, which could compromise its integrity over time. Unless it's being captured in barrels, rainwater should flow away from the house rather than seep right down the foundation walls.

If you lack the ability to set up gutters and rain barrels, all is not lost. You can still collect quite a bit of rainwater with a little planning. This technique was taught to me by John McCann at Survival Resources (SurvivalResources.com):

You'll need four metal fence posts, the kind usually used for temporary fencing, a waterproof tarp, a sledgehammer, some rope, and a few buckets. Oh, and a fist-sized rock.

Choose a location that is out in the open, not near any trees or structures. Place the tarp on the ground and stretch it out flat. Assuming the tarp is a rectangle, pound in a fence post at the two corners on a short side. Pound them deep enough to be stable and secure. Tie the corners of the tarp to the posts about 4 feet up from the ground.

At the other end, pound the posts into the ground about 1 foot in from each of the corners. For example, if your tarp is 8 feet across on the short side, your posts will be 6 feet apart. Tie the tarp to the posts a little bit lower. You'll notice that the tarp naturally creates sort of a funnel shape between those posts. You want the bottom of that funnel to be about 2 feet from the ground.

Put a bucket under the funnel and tie the fist-sized rock to the tarp at that point, letting it dangle down into the bucket. The idea is to pull the tarp down at that spot. Once it starts to rain, have multiple buckets ready to go as they will fill quickly with this setup. Swap them out as they fill up, and dump the water into a larger storage container.

If you live in an urban area, check the rooftops of buildings to see if there is a rainwater catchment system in place. Some buildings have them as part of a fire suppression system. Others funnel the rainwater down into cisterns where the water is stored for a variety of uses.

The water collected through any of these rainwater catchment systems will still need to be filtered and disinfected prior to consumption. While rain is generally pure as it falls from the sky, it can and will be contaminated by whatever it lands on.

WILD WATER SOURCES

Rivers, streams, lakes, and ponds are all potential sources of water, as long as you keep in mind a few caveats. First, odds are you aren't the only person who knows about them. I don't know that you'll need to go to battle with someone who is claiming the entire water source as their own (unless it lies completely on their own property, then you might indeed have a fight on your hands), but if your plan is to avoid all human contact, these wild sources of water might not be the way to go.

Second, you will need to make double-damn sure you do everything feasible to filter and disinfect the water prior to it crossing your lips. Waterborne pathogens such as giardia are not be to be trifled with. I don't care how pristine and clear the water looks, odds are there are going to be nasties floating in it, way too small to see and just waiting for some hapless goof to down a quart so they can go to work.

As noted earlier, water is heavy. Transporting it by hand over any sort of distance will get tiresome. But, if that's the only source of water available, you'll have to figure out a way to deal with it. One option that might be worth exploring is to use buckets with tight-fitting lids, such as the ubiquitous five-gallon pails found at any deli or bakery. Stack them two or three high on a two-wheeled dolly and cart them back and forth. A wheelbarrow might work as well but will require a bit more strength for lifting.

If the path to and from the water source is too uneven for wheeled transport, you might fashion together a shoulder pole, also known as a milkmaid's yoke. This device has been in use for thousands of years and is still being used today. It is merely a pole that is about four feet in length and rests across the back of your shoulders, with a bucket suspended at each end. The pole will need to be rather strong to support the weight of a couple buckets of water. It isn't the worst idea, either, to cut small notches at each end of the pole to prevent the bucket handles from sliding off. Use a towel or some other padding to make a cushion at the back of your neck. Lift with your knees, not your back.

Flowing water, such as streams and rivers, is generally going to be safer than standing water. Moving water won't usually be full of algae and such. But, if a still pond is your only feasible option, so be it. If you can, brush aside any thick algae growth on the water's surface before you fill your bucket. All you're really trying to do is limit the amount of material that will need to be filtered out later.

FILTRATION AND DISINFECTION

Unless you are absolutely certain the water is potable, you're going to need to filter and/or disinfect it prior to consumption or using it for food preparation. Neglecting this step can lead to serious illness or worse.

Cryptosporidium and *Giardia* are two protozoa that may be present in questionable water. Either of them can lead to gastrointestinal illness, such as vomiting or diarrhea. Other potential nasties include bacteria such as *Salmonella* or *E. coli*, and viruses like hepatitis A or enterovirus. Ingesting any of these will cause a bad day to get oh so much worse.

There are a few different approaches to consider when it comes to rendering questionable water potable. From a long-term emergency perspective, the main problem with most of them is that they aren't feasible for working on large quantities of water at once. Realistically, though, that just means that you'll need to get into the habit of cleaning your water on a regular basis so you have a constant supply on hand.

Two methods are available for rendering water potable. *Filtration* is removing the microorganisms and other potentially harmful things from the water. *Disinfection* is killing or otherwise rendering inert the bad critters and such. This is an important distinction to make as some methods won't work on some of the bad stuff. For example, some filters work great for removing sediment and debris, but they won't do anything about viruses. On the other hand, boiling water will kill biological contaminants, but it isn't going to get rid of heavy metals.

FILTRATION

While there are DIY approaches to water filtration, none of them are foolproof, and they will leave you at risk for getting sick. Whenever possible, it is best to utilize a commercial filter, one that you know to be reliable.

The Sawyer MINI is considered by many survival instructors to be the gold standard in point-of-use water filters. It will remove 99.9999 percent of all waterborne protozoa and 99.99999 percent of bacteria. It even works on microplastics, not to mention dirt and debris.

While the MINI is typically used by hikers and campers, either attached to a water bottle or affixed to a hydration pack, Sawyer offers several other products that operate on a larger scale. This includes gravity-fed models that will filter water while you attend to other things. With routine care and minimal maintenance, these filters will clean up to 100,000 gallons of water. They are also fairly inexpensive, and you could easily lie in a lifetime supply of them for not much money. At the time of this writing, a MINI runs a hair over twenty dollars or so.

If you want to move up a spot or two and get a filtration system that's truly set up for the long haul, check out the JUVO Group Water Filter. Manufactured by the people at SHTFandGO.com, it is a pump-style filter. So, while you need to operate it manually, it will remove just about anything in the water that could hurt you, including protozoa, bacteria, heavy metals, sediments, chemicals, and more. It is designed for hard use. However, the cost is considerably higher than even a handful of Sawyer MINI filters.

You can improve the efficiency, as well as the lifespan, of any filtration system by running the water through a pre-filter, such as a T-shirt or other fabric, that will trap and remove the larger things like bugs, bits of bark, and even some of the dirt and debris.

DISINFECTION

Boiling is the most foolproof way to make questionable water safe to drink. Various sources will tell you that the water needs to boil for one minute, five minutes, ten minutes, even twenty minutes or more, to make sure the tiny critters floating in it are killed. Here's the thing. If you bring water to 150°F and keep it there for at least six minutes, the water is pasteurized. That means any harmful microorganisms have been killed.

Now, the boiling point of water at sea level is 212°F. This means that by the time the water has reached a full boil, it has been well over 150°F for several minutes. As you may recall from middle school science class, the boiling point of water goes down as you move up in elevation. Meaning, it will reach a boil quicker as you increase your elevation above sea level. So, if you live significantly above sea level, you might be concerned about this whole boiling point thing. Here's where it gets interesting. The highest point on Earth is Mt. Everest. The boiling point there?

154°F. So, even if you somehow decided to bug out to the peak of the tallest mountain on the planet, you could still make your water safe to drink by just bringing it to a boil for a bit.

What you might consider doing is working this method into the daily routine of post-collapse life. For example, any time a fire is made for cooking, put on a pot of water to boil. If you're using a wood stove or fireplace for heat, put some water on to boil while you're warming up your home. This has an added benefit of adding moisture to the air. Many people will notice the dryness in the air after using wood heat for long periods of time.

Water purification tablets have a very limited shelf life, especially once the package has been opened. They really aren't suitable for those planning for long-term situations. Bleach falls into this same category, with a shelf life of less than a year.

You can, however, make a form of bleach using pool shock, and then use that to treat water. The chemical you're after is called calcium hypochlorite. Look for a package that shows at least 68 percent of that active ingredient. It is important to know that this must be stored in nonmetallic containers and should be kept cool and dry.

To make your water-treatment solution, take 1 teaspoon of pool shock and add it to 1 gallon of water. Use a plastic bottle that you can easily pour, rather than just a bucket, and label it prominently so no one mistakes it for something else. Close the bottle and shake it well to mix the water and shock together.

To purify water using this solution, you need to add it in a ratio of one part solution to 100 parts water. On the surface, that can be confusing and difficult to calculate. Here's how to make it easier. One gallon of water is 128 ounces. So, you'll need to add 1.28 ounces of your solution to it. Round it off to 1.3 ounces and you're good to go. Pour it in, stir or swirl the water to mix it a bit, and let it sit for about 30 minutes. You should smell a faint scent of chlorine in the water. If not, do it all again.

Another option for disinfecting water is distillation. Basically, this involves capturing steam from boiling water and condensing it back into liquid form. Homemade methods rarely produce enough water consistently to truly be useful, though. If you want to explore this option, I'd suggest you invest in a commercial water distiller, such as the Gravi-Stil from SHTFandGO.com.

One more great way to disinfect water is to use ultraviolet rays. Two methods use this approach. The passive method is called solar disinfection (SODIS). The active method is to use a device such as those produced by SteriPEN.

SODIS takes time but works all by itself. All you do is set it up and let the sun do all the heavy lifting. Plus, this is one way you can disinfect larger quantities of water at once. Start with plastic bottles—clear, not green. Remove all the labeling, as you want nothing to inhibit the sun's UV rays from penetrating the bottle and disinfecting the water. Fill the bottles with filtered water. The water should be as clear as possible, as any debris or sediment will likewise prevent the sun from doing its job properly.

Find a spot in your yard that gets plenty of sun. A rooftop is even better, provided you can access it safely. Lay the bottles on their sides on a dark surface. Corrugated metal works well, if available. If not, even black construction paper will work. Let the bottles sit in the sun for one full day, provided the sky is fairly clear. If you're stuck with cloudy skies, go two days. The corrugated metal or dark surface helps heat the water, which assists the overall disinfecting process.

SteriPEN is probably the best-known name in portable UV disinfection products. These products fall into two basic types: those that use batteries and those that are crank powered. Just a short burst of UV rays from one of these units will disinfect your water. No muss, no fuss. I suggest the crank-powered model, as you won't need to stock up on batteries. This technology is essentially the same as that currently used for water treatment in many major cities, just downsized for portability.

¤ ¤ ¤ ¤

Water is a precious resource, necessary for life. Plan ahead to have plenty of water stored as well as multiple means of filtering and disinfecting water from other sources.

CHAPTER 3

FOOD: HOW TO AVOID A STARVATION DIET

For the first week or so, it was like there was a neighborhood party every night. People were clearing out their refrigerators and freezers, trying to get everything cooked on the grill before it went bad. Some had more and some had less, but everyone had at least something they could contribute to the get-togethers.

Today, we'd give almost anything to have a fraction of what was eaten at just one of those impromptu backyard feasts. The thought of biting into a juicy cheeseburger or tucking into a plate of barbecued chicken wings is, at times, almost sexual in its urgency, in its lust. We aren't starving, not in a Third World sense at least, but we've all lost a fair amount of weight. Granted, for many of us that hasn't been all bad, as we had a bit extra around the middle in the first place.

Rather than the wide range of food we once enjoyed, we're now limited to whatever was picked or caught that day for dinner that night. Few of us have much left in the way of packaged foods, though I suspect a couple of the families have much larger pantries than they are letting on. Can't say I blame them for not opening their doors and letting folks have free rein. Still, it would be nice if they'd share a little with the rest of us.

Most of us are just now starting to see some results from the makeshift gardens we put in a few months back. Not a lot but enough to keep us from eating shoe-leather soup. I'm not sure what we're going to do through the winter, though.

Food is vital; that should go without saying. Without fuel, your body won't function properly, if at all. Unlike water, the odds of food falling from the sky are pretty darn remote. But the thought of trying to stockpile enough food to feed just one person for a year or more, let alone an entire family, is just not feasible nor practical for most folks. Even if you could afford the expense, where would you keep it all?

Sure, you can mitigate part of the storage problem by investing in a few pallets of freeze-dried food. It's a great way to cram a lot of calories into a small space. But here's something you'll never see mentioned in the catalogs or on the websites of companies who sell freeze-dried foods: A steady diet of that stuff will wreak havoc on your digestive tract. Not to mention the high sodium content in many of them will increase your blood pressure and have other nasty effects. Your belly will be full, but the rest of you will be falling apart.

As with most other things, you'll be best served by not putting all your eggs into one basket (no pun intended) and by diversifying your food plans. The options include food storage, growing and raising food, and finding natural sources of food through scrounging, hunting, fishing, and trapping. We'll explore each of these options, along with food preservation and cooking methods, in a bit more detail.

FOOD STORAGE

Earlier, I said that storing enough food for a year isn't practical for most folks. While true, you should still have at least some amount of food squirreled away for an emergency. When preparing for long-term events, your minimum goal for food storage should be three months. Supplemented with wild edibles, garden produce, and other items, this stockpile should be able to stretch to six months or more. The idea behind having some amount of stored food is to give you a cushion. If the garden doesn't produce enough due to weather issues, or the local pond gets fished out quickly, you have something to fall back on until you can get over the proverbial hump.

Stored food should include a combination of canned or boxed goods as well as dry grains, pasta, and legumes. You want a wide variety of foods, if at all possible. You should also concentrate on the foods your family enjoys eating. Here are a few examples:

RICE: Stick with white rice varieties as the husk on brown rice will go rancid.

BEANS: These are a great protein source when meat isn't an option.

CANNED AND POUCH MEATS: When the hunting and trapping isn't going well, you can still put together a decent meal.

DRY PASTA: Kept dry, this lasts just about forever. It's a great filler, too.

CANNED VEGETABLES AND FRUITS: While not as good as fresh, they'll still provide necessary vitamins and nutrients. Most canned goods will store well for at least a year or more, provided they are kept cool and dry. This is why you should store only the foods your family currently eats, as you'll want to rotate out the canned goods before they reach their expiration dates. Any cans you pull from the pantry that are bulging or rusted should be tossed.

THE IMPORTANCE OF DIVERSIFICATION

In early 2014, a chemical spill in West Virginia left about 300,000 people unable to use their tap water for virtually anything. The chemical, 4-methylcyclohexane methanol, which is used in the coal industry, leaked into the Elk River from a processing plant. From there, it worked its way into city water systems. Within hours of the spill's announcement, there wasn't a bottle of water nor bag of ice to be had anywhere in the area.

This is something to keep in mind as you plan your food storage. Many long-term foods marketed to preppers require the addition of water to make the food palatable. This is all well and good when water is in large supply. But the wise survivalist diversifies their food storage to include things that are ready to eat, right out of the can or bag.

SOUPS AND STEWS: Odds are pretty good you'll be making a lot of soups and stews due to their simplicity. Basically, you add whatever food you have to a pot of water and let it cook down a bit. Bouillon cubes will help dramatically with making your soups more flavorful. Dehydrated soup mixes, the type that are sold in pouches, are another excellent option. They will keep just about forever and, provided you have the water needed to cook, make quite a bit. My family particularly likes the Shore Lunch soup mixes. One pouch will make, on average, about eight cups of soup.

BAKING MIXES: Don't forget to add baking mixes to your storage. Look for the varieties that require only the addition of water, as opposed to milk, eggs, and shortening. A hearty bean stew coupled with a plate of hot biscuits makes for a great meal.

COOKING OILS: Stick with the vegetable oils rather than lard or shortening as they will store longer. Oils will provide necessary fats in your diet.

SPROUTS: These are incredibly high in nutrients and easy to grow. Although you can sprout a variety of seeds and beans, the milder flavors come from mung beans, alfalfa, and clover. Rinse the seeds in clean water, then put them in a clear jar and soak overnight. Drain the water (reusing it in the garden rather than wasting it) and then keep the seeds moist by rinsing and draining them two or three times a day. In three to five days, you'll have a new crop of sprouts to add to salads or to eat as a side dish. You can get the appropriate seeds or beans at health food stores. They should come with any special instructions that might apply.

HERBS AND SPICES: In addition to storing foods, don't forget about things like herbs, spices, and gravy mixes that will all help with making the food more palatable. If you aren't very experienced with cooking from scratch, take the time to learn now, rather than having to puzzle it out while your hungry family is staring at you, hoping for something that is at least somewhat edible.

GROWING AND RAISING FOOD

When the cars stop working and shouting over fences replaces email, many backyards will be turned into garden plots. I firmly believe that just about everyone can produce at least some amount of food, no matter where they live. It is just a matter of exploring different options and perhaps using some creativity. Of course, if the grid goes down for a long period of time, some approaches that are forbidden today might become acceptable, such as current prohibitions by some homeowner's associations against growing gardens.

GARDENING

Survivalists often overlook the fact that growing a garden is an awful lot of work, especially if you're starting from scratch. There seems to be a mentality out there that one merely needs to stockpile a bunch of seeds and, when the time comes, toss them into the ground and wait for food to appear. Reality is far different.

I'm not suggesting you abandon plans to produce food for your family using gardens. What I am saying, though, is that you should start now rather than waiting until you truly need that food to survive.

Invest in a large quantity of *heirloom seeds*. For those not in the know, heirloom seeds are those that will breed true, meaning you can grow a tomato plant, then take seeds from the fruit (yes, tomatoes are indeed a fruit, not a vegetable) and grow more tomatoes. Most of the seeds you find at discount stores and the like are hybrids. There is a risk with hybrid seeds in that they may not breed true or perhaps not grow at all. Heirloom seeds are more expensive than hybrids but are definitely worth the price. Some great sources for heirloom seeds include:

BAKER CREEK HEIRLOOM SEEDS: RareSeeds.com

SEEDS FOR GENERATIONS: SeedsforGenerations.com

SEED SAVERS EXCHANGE: SeedSavers.org

DIY SEED TAPE

Many seeds are extremely small. As a result, traditional methods of planting generally result in waste. For example, carrot seeds are very tiny. Many gardeners will just scatter a line of seeds in a small trench and then thin out seedlings that sprout to prevent overcrowding.

Seed tape is a great way to prevent that waste. Basically, it is a strip of material with seeds affixed at specific intervals. You plant the strip and up come the seedlings with plenty of room for growing between them. Seed tape can be pricey, though, so here's a way to make it yourself.

For this project, you'll need seeds, flour, water, toilet paper, a ruler, a pen or marker, paper plate, and toothpicks.

Start by making a glue by mixing two parts flour with one part water. You don't need much, just a tablespoon of flour and ½ tablespoon water will probably suffice. Roll out about 12 to 18 inches of toilet paper and tear it off the roll. Fold the toilet paper in half lengthwise, then open it back up.

Follow the seed package's recommendations for spacing. Use the ruler and pen to make a small mark where the seeds will be placed. Put the marks on the lower half of the strip of toilet paper, roughly in the middle of that section.

Shake out the seeds onto a paper plate. Dip a toothpick into the glue, then use it to pick up one seed. Wipe the seed along with the glue dollop on one of the marks on the toilet paper. Repeat until each mark is covered with a seed.

Fold the toilet paper over and seal each end with a couple of small dots of glue. Label each strip you do by writing on the end of it. Let the strips dry overnight, then store them in sealed plastic bags. Be sure to label each strip using a pen or marker.

Knowing how to save and preserve seeds from one harvest to the next season is important. It makes little sense to invest in heirloom seeds if you let the seeds from the resulting crop spoil or rot.

SEED STORAGE

It is critical to properly save seeds so they are available the next growing season. As discussed previously, if you start with heirloom varieties of crops, you'll be able to plant the seeds from the fruits and vegetables you harvest and have them grow properly.

Storing seeds for long-term use does take a little time and effort, but it is necessary so you will be in a position to be able to feed your family the following year. Remember, this isn't anything new or revolutionary. Rather, we're just going back to the way things used to be done.

The enemies of seed storage are the same as with storing just about anything—heat, sunlight, and moisture. Avoid storing them where the temperatures fluctuate, such as an outbuilding or garage. The ideal storage temperature is 40°F, though that might not be feasible for everyone. Even a standard basement is better than keeping them at room temperature all year long.

If you do store seeds in the refrigerator or freezer, let them come back up to room temperature while still in the sealed container before you open it. This prevents condensation from forming inside the container and possibly fouling the seed packets.

SEED COLLECTION

The first step of seed collection is to remove the seeds from the plant. Sometimes, as in the case of pumpkins, for example, the seeds are pretty easy to find. With others, such as carrots, the seed pod isn't attached to the fruit or vegetable, and you'll need to know what it looks like and where to find it. Yet one more reason why it is important to get started with gardening before it comes time to rely on your harvest for survival.

If the seeds are dry, shake them into an envelope or other container. I cannot stress enough the importance of properly labeling all seed containers immediately. It is far too easy to get distracted and then forget which container has which seeds. Even writing it on a strip of masking tape with a pen will be sufficient for the time being.

Wet seeds, such as those collected from pumpkins or squash, must be dried before storage. Toss them into a bowl and fill the bowl with water. Any seeds that float are dead and can be tossed into compost. Swish your hand through the seeds in the water several times to clean them off, then carefully pour out the water and the bits of pulp. Lay the seeds out to dry for several days. Old plastic cutting boards or baking sheets work great for this purpose.

Once the seeds are dry, they can go into a properly labeled container.

DRYING SEEDS FOR STORAGE

Yes, we just talked about cleaning and drying seeds. There's a difference between drying and *drying*. If you plan on keeping seeds for more than a year or so, they need to be properly dried. What we want to do is remove moisture without heating the seeds. Hot temperatures may kill the seeds, which renders this whole process moot.

One approach is to simply leave the seeds out on baking sheets or something similar and let evaporation do the job, as described above. This will work, but it can be a pain to have countless sheets of seeds occupying several shelves and taking up valuable counter space in the kitchen. There's the risk of insects or critters getting at the seeds, too. Fortunately, there are other options.

A great way to dry seeds for storage is to use the cell phone approach. What is one of the most commonly suggested remedies if you drop your cell phone in water? Stick it in a bag of rice for a couple of days, right? Rice absorbs moisture like that's its job and it is going for employee of the month. The same principle will work with drying seeds.

Stop in at your local dollar store and pick up some nylons. Cut them into sections to make small pouches. The foot part is easy—just snip it off. For the remainder of the nylon, which amounts to a series of tubes, just knot one end of each section. Fill these pouches with seeds, being very careful to keep track of what seeds are in each pouch, then knot them closed. Keep the knots somewhat loose so you can untie them easily.

Fill a jar about halfway with rice, place a few pouches of seeds inside, then cover with rice and close the jar. The seeds should be sufficiently dried in a couple of weeks.

If you have a vacuum sealer, use it to remove the air from the seed containers before storing them. Otherwise, put the seeds into plastic bags and squeeze as much air out of them as you can. Many gardeners store seeds in the freezer. After a grid collapse, though, you'll need to come up with a different plan. A container that is relatively rodent and insect-proof, such as a cooler, can work great. Keep it in a cool and dark location.

One more thing with labeling your seeds: consider writing down the planting instructions for each type of seed and placing that note with the seeds. This way, there will hopefully be no confusion when it comes time to plant. While you might know this information off the top of your head, others in the family might not and, well, there's always a chance that you won't be the one doing the planting in the future.

DRYING RICE

Because rice absorbs moisture so readily, it may already have a small amount of water inside and, thus, may not be quite the desiccant it could otherwise be. You can cure this problem by baking the rice for 35 to 45 minutes at 350°F. This isn't absolutely necessary, but if you have the means to easily accomplish it, go ahead. Transfer the rice right from the oven into a jar and seal it so no moisture can get inside. Wait until the rice is cool before using it to dry seeds or your cell phone.

GARDEN JOURNAL

As you progress through your journey into gardening, you might want to make notes in a journal. Keep track of information like what you planted, when you started the seeds, and when the sprouts came up. Make a few notes on the prevailing weather conditions, too, such as periods of heavy rain or drought.

By keeping track of how well or poorly each crop does, along with the weather conditions and such, you'll be able to at least somewhat accurately predict how future crops will do.

The garden journal need not be anything fancy. Just a standard spiral notebook will suffice. It is important, though, that it be a hard copy journal, not just a file kept on the computer. If the grid goes down, it'll be rather difficult to access that information otherwise.

Add a section to your garden journal for notes on your seed storage. Keep track of what seeds you set aside each season, maybe with a description or photo in case a container's label disappears.

CHOOSING THE GARDEN LOCATION

A successful garden needs sun, water, and good soil. As you determine the best location for your garden, keep these three elements in mind.

Most garden plants need full sun, meaning strong sunlight for at least six hours each day. If you're unsure whether a certain spot in your yard will work, stand out there facing south (assuming you're in the northern hemisphere). Stretch out your arms to either side. Your left arm is pointed roughly east and your right arm roughly west. As the sun moves throughout the day, it will do so in an arc in front of where you're standing. Are there any large buildings, trees, or other obstacles that would throw shade on your potential garden plot? If so, you'll either need to move the plot or move the obstruction. If neither of those are options, you'll have to make do and hope for the best. As long as the plants get a few hours of sun each day, they should do okay.

Proximity to your water source is important as well. While gardeners do treasure regular rainfall, there are going to be times when you'll need to water the crops by hand. If you'll be carrying buckets of water from rain barrels or another source, keep in mind that water is heavy. The shorter the traveling distance, the better. Helpful hint: It is actually easier to carry a bucket of water in each hand than it is to carry one bucket at a time. Two buckets balance the load.

As for soil, you probably have a little work ahead of you.

SOIL AMENDMENTS

Few backyards have soil that is perfect for gardening without some assistance. The best soil is filled with nutrients and feels light and perhaps a little fluffy. If you squeeze your fist around a handful, it will retain that shape when you open your hand, then slowly expand back to its original shape. Odds are that doesn't accurately describe what is under the grass outside your back door.

HOW IMPORTANT IS IT TO BE ORGANIC?

One of the most popular buzzwords for the last several years is *organic*. In general, it refers to garden practices that are free from chemicals like pesticides. Like vegetarianism, there are varying degrees of what might be allowed and still be termed organic. I'm not going to tell you all pesticides are horrible, and I'm not going to tell you to stock up on herbicides and other mixtures that are filled with ingredients few people can pronounce correctly.

At home, we try to avoid adding chemicals to our garden as best we can. However, we are guilty of using Miracle-Gro from time to time. Using pesticides and other such products is a judgment call. Remember, though, that if a long-term disaster were to come to pass, access to those products will likely be nonexistent outside what you have stored at home.

More common issues with soil include being too sandy or having an abundance of clay. Sandy soil feels very gritty, and you can often see the sand mixed in with the black dirt. Clay soil is sticky when wet and very hard when dry.

Sandy soil tends to be easy to dig, which is a good thing, but it often lacks the nutrients plants need to thrive. Clay is often filled with great nutrients, but they are locked into the soil as water isn't able to penetrate it easily.

Fortunately, the remedy is the same for both. Adding organic material to the soil will improve the situation dramatically. Compost and rotted manure will add nutrients to the soil as well as provide enough water retention for the plants to absorb the nutrients and minerals.

COMPOST

One of the very best soil amendments is also one of the easiest to procure. Compost is simply vegetable scraps and fruit peels from the kitchen, grass clippings, and other organic material that is left to decompose. Basically, anything that was or was part of a plant can go into the compost pile or bin. This includes things like coffee grounds and tea. Even egg shells can be added to the compost. Avoid meats, grease, and pet feces.

Gardeners classify compost ingredients into two categories: brown and green. The general rule of thumb is three parts brown ingredients to one part green ingredient.

Green Compost
- grass clippings
- vegetable scraps
- fruit peels
- coffee grounds

Brown Compost
- newspapers
- cardboard
- leaves
- pine needles
- sawdust (from untreated lumber)

Honestly, though, we haven't paid very close attention to the ratio at home. When we have kitchen scraps, they go into one of our compost bins. When we use the bagger attachment on our mower, which we don't do every time we mow but just when the grass is exceptionally long, the clippings go into a compost bin. If the bins are getting really gooey from all the fresh greens that are decaying, we'll add in some shredded newspaper.

If you are starting a compost pile for the first time, scatter in a few shovelfuls of dirt. This adds microscopic organisms that will aid in the composting process.

The thing about compost is that the ingredients will decay whether you do anything with them or not. You can just leave it all in a pile in the backyard, and sooner or later, it'll turn into compost. Most gardeners, though, want that "black gold" sooner rather than later. To help speed the process along, add air and water on a regular basis.

When adding water, don't drench the pile but give it a good drink, sprinkling the entire surface of the pile. Turn the pile after doing so. Use a pitchfork or other tool to shift everything around, allowing some air to get inside the pile. Do this every week or two, especially if the pile is exposed to the elements and there has been a good rain. Of course, you could always get a tumbler compost bin. These are barrels that are designed to roll easily, allowing you to mix the compost ingredients without a backache.

Retailers sell compost bins in a wide range of sizes and shapes. A simple pile in the corner of the yard will work just fine, though. Or, craft your own bin from pallets and chicken wire. The purpose of a bin is merely to keep the materials contained as they turn to compost.

You can make compost in small amounts, too, rather than using just one large pile. One method uses black garbage bags. Add in one part brown material, one part green material, and one part soil. Dampen the whole mess with water, seal the bag, then put it into a second bag and seal that as well. Let this sit for anywhere from six weeks to six months. Yes, results vary that widely. Turn the bag over about every two weeks and check it at the six-week mark. If it doesn't look and smell like compost, close it back up and check again in a few weeks. Store the bags outdoors in the summer and bring them into a heated part of the house in the winter. The nice thing about this method is it allows you to create compost all year long.

MANURE

Never add fresh manure to the garden. It will shock the plants and possibly add pathogens to the mix, which isn't a good thing. Age manure for about six months. If you have the space and the supplies, make a pile just for manure and mix it with straw or newspaper. It takes several months to ensure any nasty stuff has been killed off before you can safely add it to the garden. The exception to this rule is rabbit manure. That can be added to the garden without being aged.

Keep the pile well away from food and water sources.

HUMANURE

You can compost human waste, should you so desire. Basically, this entails using a receptacle like a 5-gallon bucket to collect the feces and urine. The waste is eventually dumped into a compost heap and covered with hay, straw, or weeds. Humanure proponents suggest composting everything together, from human waste to kitchen scraps to newspapers and such. One of the top authoritative texts on the subject is *The Humanure Handbook: A Guide to Composting Human Manure*, 3rd Edition, by Joseph C. Jenkins (Grove City, PA: Joseph Jenkins, Inc., 2005).

VERMICULITE

Vermiculite is a mineral that is sold in bags in some garden stores. In some areas, it can be difficult to find, so you might want to call ahead or order online. It is often used as a soil additive to help aerate the soil as well as improve its water retention. Basically, vermiculite will absorb water like tiny sponges and then slowly release it, allowing you to go a little longer between watering the garden. It also helps to break up the soil and allows it to drain better.

Perlite is a somewhat similar material but many gardeners feel it is a poor substitute for vermiculite.

MEL'S MIX

Mel Bartholomew has been at the forefront of the Square Foot Gardening movement for many years. He wrote a great book on the subject, aptly titled *All New Square Foot Gardening*. One of the things he talks about is a special mixture he concocted as a growing medium. The idea is to forgo using dirt completely and just use this mix.

The recipe is pretty simple: one part vermiculite, one part peat moss, and one part compost. The idea for this combination is great water and nutrient retention coupled with a light and airy medium that allows roots to grow easily.

While many gardeners swear by this mix, others have modified it here and there, such as reducing the vermiculite and adding more compost, to suit their own needs. After all, vermiculite costs money and compost can be made for free at home.

Given that our focus here is on a long-term grid-down situation, we cannot assume mass quantities of such soil amendments would be readily available. With that in mind, here are two suggestions: First, try different mix ratios, including native soil or even bagged topsoil, to see what works best for your area. Second, if you find you have great success with the addition of one or more soil amendments, consider stocking up extra bags for the long haul, just in case.

PEAT MOSS

Another common soil additive is peat moss. This is sphagnum moss that has died and decayed. It acts like a sponge to soak up water and release it to the growing plants as needed. It also helps prevent nutrients in the soil from washing away when the plants are watered. Peat moss is usually sold in compressed packages and will expand when the package is opened.

CONTAINER GARDENING

If you lack space for an actual in-the-ground garden, container gardening might be the way to go. This is also a great option for those who live in an area governed by a homeowner's association that has rules against large gardens.

Container gardening is simply growing your crops in pots and planters rather than in the ground. One advantage to this approach is you can move the planters throughout the day to maximize their exposure to the sun. Plus, you can put the containers up on benches or even tables so there's no stooping or bending involved when weeding or harvesting.

You'll typically need far less soil and water for a container garden than a traditional one, too, which is something to consider if the supply of either of those is threatened.

You could easily line your patio, deck, or even driveway with a series of pots and planters and grow quite a bit of food throughout the season. The downside, though, is that you're limited to what you can grow by the size of the containers available. I mean, you're not going to be growing very much corn or wheat in planters sitting on the deck. But for a lot of the standard garden fare, from carrots to radishes, peppers to tomatoes, container gardening works very well.

When the grid goes down, possibly permanently, consider using container gardening to supplement any traditional gardens you plant.

RAISED BEDS

Raised-bed gardening is like container gardening taken to the next level. It is sort of a step between container gardening and traditional gardens. The basic concept is to build boxes that rest on the ground, fill the boxes with prepared soil or a growing medium, and plant your seeds. This is an excellent option for those who have poor soil in their yards. Rather than tilling up entire sections of the yard, you just need to put the boxes down where you want them and fill them up.

There are many ways to go about building raised beds, some far more complicated and involved than others. Start with determining the materials you'll use to build the walls of the bed. Lumber is the most common, but people have used brick, stone, or even logs. If you opt for boards, avoid using any lumber that has been treated with toxins to preserve them. Those chemicals can leach into the soil and thus into whatever you're growing. Use cedar or another naturally weather-resistant wood. Galvanized steel screws are advisable, too.

The total growing space in the raised bed should be about a foot or so deep. This gives roots plenty of space. Keep this in mind as you design your raised bed. The walls of the bed will determine how much soil and, thus, growing space you'll have inside the bed. Note that you won't be filling the bed to the top with soil, either. Typically, the raised bed is filled to a few inches from the top of the frame.

Decide where in the yard you're going to put the raised beds. Use stakes and string to outline each bed. Remove the turf as well as at least the first few inches of dirt from within the space. Then, assemble and install the raised bed. The sides of the bed should be at least a few inches in the ground. Some gardeners recommend lining the bottom of the bed with hardware cloth or something similar to discourage pests like moles from taking an underground path to your food. We haven't had that problem in any of our raised beds, but your mileage, as they say, may vary.

You might consider adding some reinforcement to the sides of the bed to prevent them from sagging under the expansion of the dirt inside. Pound stakes or rebar along the sides of the bed, being sure to drive the tops down past the upper edges so you don't catch on them as you're weeding and such.

Fill the bed with your prepared soil or growing medium, such as Mel's Mix, and you're ready to go.

COLD FRAMES AND GREENHOUSES

The length of the growing season varies throughout the country. The season gets shorter the further north you go. On top of that, at least a couple of different potential long-term disasters, such as a massive volcanic eruption that affects the amount of sunlight reaching the Earth's surface for months or even years, would seriously mess with the growing season.

You can offset this a bit and take advantage of the sun's energy to increase or extend the growing season through the use of cold frames, hoop houses, and greenhouses.

COLD FRAME

After a major event, the structures in the area are likely to suffer some damage. Any intact windows should be salvaged and put to use. A cold frame is simply an insulated box with a window for a lid. The window allows the sun's energy to heat the interior of the box and the insulation keeps the heat there.

A cold frame is typically constructed out of lumber with the overall size matching the window being used for the top. For convenience, this window is usually attached to the box with hinges, but this isn't absolutely necessary. The box is usually made so the window is set at an angle to allow for maximum sun exposure.

The traditional insulation for a cold frame is bales of hay stacked around it. In fact, the simplest way to make a cold frame is to use four bales of hay to create the box, and placing the window on top.

Use the cold frame in the early spring and in the fall but refrain from keeping plants in one during the summer. The inside of the cold frame will get very hot in the summer and could kill the plants.

GREENHOUSE

A greenhouse works on the same principle as the cold frame. It gathers energy from the sun to heat the interior. Greenhouses come in all shapes and sizes and are typically made from either glass or plastic sheeting. Some are truly elaborate affairs, complete with heaters to use in the winter, large fans for air movement, and other amenities.

If enough windows can be salvaged or scrounged, a greenhouse could be cobbled together fairly easily by anyone with rudimentary carpentry skills. It may not be pretty, but as long as it is functional, who cares?

It is important to allow for some air flow through the greenhouse during the warmer months, lest it get downright unbearable inside. Either make sure some of the windows can be opened or allow for a means to prop open the door.

HOOP HOUSE

A hoop house is truly just another form of greenhouse, albeit one that is pretty easy to put together with materials found at any hardware store. Gardeners who make use of hoop houses will often build them right over their garden beds. There are a few different ways to build a hoop house, but the basics are fairly similar.

While the supplies could likely be scrounged later, it pays to plan ahead and invest in the materials while they are easy to find. The hoop house described here is very basic, with no frills like doors and such. It will do the job as is but if you're the handy sort I'm sure you will want to embellish the design a bit.

The exact measurements for this project will depend on the garden plot you're covering. For the purposes of our discussion, we'll say the plot is 10 feet long and 4 feet wide. Once you understand the basic construction, you can easily adapt it to suit your needs. Obviously, the quantity of the PVC tubing, rebar, and other materials will depend upon the size of the hoop house you're building.

You'll need:

- 2 x 6' boards (weather-resistant)
- stainless steel screws
- 36" rebar
- hammer or sledgehammer
- 10' x ¾" PVC tubing
- ¾" conduit straps
- 6 mil plastic sheeting
- zip ties
- wood lathe
- long staples
- staple gun
- drill

Build a frame around the perimeter of the garden by placing the boards on their sides, cutting them to fit, and screwing them together at the corners. Measure the two diagonal lengths. If they don't match, your corners aren't quite square, so shift things around a bit until they are.

Beginning at the corners and running the long sides of the rectangle, pound the rebar into the ground about every 2 feet. In our example, this comes to six lengths of rebar on each of the long sides of the frame. The rebar should be positioned on the outside of the boards and as close to the wood as you can get. Leave about 12 inches of rebar exposed above ground.

One at a time, slide the PVC over the rebar on one side, then bend the PVC over and slide it over the rebar on the opposite side. You'll end up with an arch about 4 feet high in the middle. Experience has taught me that this is about the highest arch you can do without needing a lot of extra support. You won't be able to stand and walk through the hoop house, but all the plants are down at ground level anyway, right?

Run one length of PVC along the top of the arch and attach it to each bent PVC with a zip tie. Be sure to position the zip tie such that the clasp is on the underside pointed into the hoop house, rather than on top. This prevents it from snagging the plastic sheeting.

Use the 3/4" conduit straps to hold the PVC against the boards. One strap on each end of the PVC should be sufficient.

If you plan to reuse the plastic sheeting from year to year, you'll have to go with 6 mil thickness. Anything thinner will not hold up to repeated use. On a day when the wind is relatively calm, unfold the plastic and drape it over the hoop house. Make sure to overlap on the long sides enough that the plastic touches the ground. On the front and back of the hoop house, leave enough excess plastic to be able to cover the opening entirely. This may mean you'll need more than one package of plastic sheeting, depending on the overall length of your hoop house. In this example, we need at least 18 feet total length and 10 feet total width.

Cut the wood lathe into pieces about 18 inches long. Beginning at one end of the hoop house, staple the lathe to the boards, trapping the plastic. Position the lathe between the PVC. Go all the way down one side of the hoop house, then go to the other side. Pull the plastic as tight as you can before stapling down the lathe. Using the lathe will make it easier to remove the staples and plastic when it comes time to take down the hoop house. You'll just pry up the lathe and the staples will come with it.

Fold the plastic at the ends of the hoop house and secure with binder clips, clothespins, or something similar. When you need to enter to the hoop house, just undo the clips and fold the plastic up over the top of the house.

CHOOSING WHAT TO PLANT

As you peruse various seed catalogs and websites, you might find the selection process daunting. There is a dizzying array of choices. Keep a couple of guidelines in mind.

PLANT WHAT YOU EAT

It makes little sense to invest time, energy, and likely already-limited resources of water and space to growing food you and your family don't like to eat. Forget any notions of "Well, if we get hungry enough...." Why inflict that misery on yourself if you don't need to do so? Sit down and make a list of the vegetables and fruits your family eats regularly. Then, do some research to determine which of them will readily grow in your area. As a general rule, if you can find it at local farm stands, you can probably grow it at home.

For the last several years, we've been experimenting a bit and have added at least one new crop to our garden each season. Some we've continued to grow, others we determined we didn't like. While times are somewhat normal, trying new things is perfectly fine. When times are rough, though, concentrate on using every bit of garden space to grow food that will not go to waste because no one wants to eat it.

COMPANION PLANTING

Companion planting is a way to take advantage of the strengths of different plants by planting them together. One example is the so-called

Three Sisters Garden. Start by making small mounds in the garden bed, each about 1 foot high and 18 inches across. The hills should be spaced about 3 feet apart. The mounds aren't absolutely necessary but they can help with water drainage. Build the mounds in a grid pattern rather than in a straight line as this will assist with pollination.

Plant three to six corn seeds in each mound, spacing them about 6 inches apart. Once those have grown to about 5 to 6 inches in height, which takes a couple of weeks, plant two to three bean seeds at the base of each corn plant. Space these about 6 inches from each other and from the corn plant. Then, about a week after that, plant five to six squash or pumpkin seeds in a circle pattern at the outskirts of each mound.

As the plants grow, the corn provides support for the beans to grow on and the pumpkin's broad leaves provide shade that conserves moisture and keeps down weeds. The pumpkin vines are also somewhat spiny, which deters critters. Many people substitute butternut squash for the pumpkins. Traditionally, it wasn't sweet corn that was used but dent corn, which is used for making corn meal. However, many people have had great success with sweet corn.

Other companion planting arrangements include:

Plant	Companions
Beets	Onions
Cabbage	Potatoes, celery, mint
Carrots	Peas, lettuce, onions, tomatoes
Cucumbers	Beans, corn, peas, radishes
Garlic	Raspberries
Radishes	Peas, lettuce, cucumbers
Strawberries	Spinach, lettuce

Use paper and pencil to make a diagram of your garden beds. Graph paper works great for this, if you have it available. Taking into account the space needs for each plant, companion planting suggestions, and the available sunlight in different parts of the garden, sketch out a map of what you'll plant where. If you're not actually planting the garden yet, keep this map with your seeds so you have it available when it is needed.

MEAT PRODUCTION

Raising food animals is also definitely something to consider. Rabbits, chickens, and even goats will do well in small areas. As with gardening, though, this isn't something you can start doing at the drop of a hat. After the grid goes down, you'll not be able to waltz down to the feed store and pick up a few chicks to raise for Sunday dinners. But if you start now, a half-dozen chickens will keep you in eggs and fresh meat for quite some time.

Raising backyard critters has become rather popular recently. Many libraries as well as community groups have begun offering free or low-cost classes to teach people how to raise small animals like rabbits, chickens, and goats, right in the city or suburb. If such classes aren't available in your area, hit the library shelves for more information.

Another food animal to consider raising is tilapia. These fish breed easily and grow to good size rather quickly. You don't need a large pond either. They will live quite well in food-grade barrels. As a bonus, the water you rotate out of the barrels is fantastic for your garden beds.

BEEKEEPING

While honey isn't something you can really live on, it is extremely healthy and an excellent substitute for sugar in most recipes. Honey contains powerful antioxidants and can also be used topically as an antiseptic on wounds. You might consider investing in a beehive to keep at the edge of your property. This is not a small investment in money nor time, but it may prove to be lucrative when it comes to bartering, which we'll discuss in a later chapter. Suffice it to say, the person who shows up to the trade with a pint of honey will probably be able to name their price.

FORAGING WILD EDIBLES

Outside the extreme northern and southern ends of the globe, wild edibles can be found just about everywhere. However, it takes time and effort to learn what foods can be foraged in your area. This isn't something you can simply grab a book on and learn in an afternoon. You can certainly start there, of course, but you need to get your butt off the couch and outside to really know what you're doing.

For beginners, I heartily recommend either Peterson's *Field Guide to Edible Wild Plants* (get the edition appropriate for your area) or *Foraging Wild Edible Plants of North America: More Than 150 Delicious Recipes Using Nature's Edibles* by Christopher Nyerges. Then, get in touch with your local county extension office and find out if they offer any courses in wild edibles. Most do offer such training at various times of the year. Go out on hikes in your area and practice identifying plants, getting to know their appearance during different seasons and at different stages of growth. Once you are comfortable identifying plants, make an effort to add them to your regular meals from time to time. This will allow you to determine which ones agree with both your palate and your digestive system.

Most people are familiar with some of the more common wild edibles like blackberries and dandelion greens. They might not regularly eat, or even think about, dandelion salad, but it is there for the taking.

While people in times past were able to live well on foraged foods, that likely won't be the case after a major disaster. Odds are pretty good that folks will be out in force, stuffing anything green into their pie holes and hoping for the best. Sure, Darwin's Law will winnow out those people eventually, but that won't make new plants grow any faster. That said, by taking the time now to learn what is good to eat and what isn't, you'll be in a better position to get out in front of the crowd.

HUNTING, FISHING, AND TRAPPING

Quite often, these pursuits form the backbone of a person's long-term survival planning. Some survivalists figure they will be able to keep their larder full by hitting the trail just a few times a week. Sure, this might work out for those who live way out in the sticks, well off the beaten path. But for those who live in cities, suburbs, or even smaller towns, the competition is going to be fierce. Expect forests to get hunted out fairly quickly; same with small lakes getting fished out.

I'm not saying you should give up all plans of augmenting your food supply with wild game. What I am saying, though, is that shouldn't be your primary plan.

TRAPPING

Of the three approaches to putting wild meat on the table, trapping is the one that requires the least amount of energy on your part. Traps will work on your behalf 24/7, though you will need to check them on a regular basis. If you are going to go this route, I suggest you plan on checking all traps at least once a day. While you don't want to spend endless hours running through your trap route, likely disturbing the very critters you want to catch, you also don't want another predator (whether on two legs or four) to find your catch before you do.

The best snares around are likely the ones produced by Thompson. They come in a few different sizes and are rather easy to set. I buy mine from Survival Resources (www.SurvivalResources.com). Notice, though, I said they are easy to set, not that they are easy to use. Trapping or snaring game has a learning curve, just like anything else. Take the time to do your homework on the types of game that live in your area. Find out what they eat, when they are most active, and where they likely make their homes. Only with this information can you make the best decisions on how and where to place the traps.

FISHING

There are certainly worse ways to spend a lazy afternoon than sitting on shore with a line in the water. But the object here isn't relaxation; it is to fill bellies. Increase your odds of success by using trotlines and automatic fishing reels.

Trotlines are simply a way to fish with several lines in the water at once. Typically, they are placed in rivers or streams, rather than lakes or ponds. A rope or other cord is run from one riverbank directly across to the other. At intervals along the way, smaller lines, called snoods, drop down into the water. Each snood ends in a baited hook. For faster-moving rivers and streams, you might affix a weight to each snood as well, to prevent the bait from rising up to the surface. It is important to keep the snoods from tangling with one another. A great way to prevent this is to space them out according to their length. For example, if you are fishing a foot down, keep the snoods three feet apart along the main line. This way, the fish you catch won't get tangled with one another. It is also a good idea to attach floats, such as empty milk jugs, to the main line to keep things from sagging too much. Check your trotline a couple times a day, if you can, to retrieve your fish and bait the hooks again.

Automatic fishing reels, sometimes called *yo-yo fishing reels*, are another way to keep fishing while you're off doing other things. These reels can be found at various sporting goods stores as well as online. Essentially, they work like, well, yo-yos. You bait the hook and drop it into the water, then attach the reel to a tree or heavy rock. If a fish gets hooked, the motion trips the reel, causing it to retract the line automatically.

Fishing is also an activity requiring homework. You need to determine which bodies of water in your area have sustainable populations of fish and what types they are. This will help you determine the best ways to catch them, such as particular baits to use and times of day best suited for fishing. The good news, though, is getting outfitted with basic fishing tackle is a rather inexpensive proposition. For example, just the other day I spent under ten bucks and came home with over fifty new hooks, about forty split-shot sinkers, and a couple spools of line. If need be, I could attach line to a branch and I'd be in business with just those supplies.

HUNTING

Now, those of you who regularly go fishing or otherwise spend a lot of time outdoors may notice that the methods I've presented thus far, trotlines and snares among them, aren't often legal in today's world, at least in most areas. I am certainly not suggesting anyone go out and incur the wrath of their local authorities. But, should there come to pass the type of long-term disaster we're focused on here, those laws will likely become moot. In fact, some current regulations, when turned around, become helpful tips and suggestions on increasing your odds of success.

For example, hunters know that in most locales, "shining" deer is forbidden. This activity consists of taking a powerful flashlight out in the wilderness. You find a meadow or field and shine the light. If you see a set of eyes reflecting back at you, aim for a spot between them with your rifle. The light not only allows you to see where the deer are located, it also tends to make them freeze upon seeing it, giving the hunter ample opportunity to line up the shot. After a societal collapse, this might be one way to dramatically increase the chances of you putting some meat on the table.

Bear in mind, though, you might not want to concentrate your hunting efforts just on big game like deer. Sure, you can secure a lot of meat with one shot, but you have to have a way to preserve that meat, otherwise it will just go to waste. My suggestion is to be prepared to hunt whatever you happen to find, from squirrel on up.

FOOD PRESERVATION

Naturally, you are going to need methods for keeping food reasonably fresh for at least a minimal length of time. Refrigerators and freezers don't work so well without power. Fortunately, there are a few other ways you can keep your food from going bad.

DEHYDRATION

Fruit, vegetables, and even meat can be dehydrated rather easily. Take a screen from one of your windows and wash it well to get rid of fly gunk and such. Slice the food about a quarter-inch thick and place in a single layer on the screen. Try to keep the slices all about the same thickness so they will dry evenly. Lay another screen on top to keep bugs off, then set it in the back window of a car parked in the sun.

When dehydrating meat, which is essentially making jerky, be sure to remove all fat from each slice. Otherwise, the fat will go rancid and spoil the meat. It is always best to use the leanest meats available when dehydrating for food storage. If you have the means to freeze the meat prior to slicing, your job will be made much easier. Of course, dried meat is best with the addition of salt and spices. I suggest you try out several different recipes and determine the ones you like the most, then stock up on the necessary spices.

Back in the old days, they would dehydrate apples simply by coring them, then cutting them into thin slices. They would then run a string through the apple slices and hang them around the house to dry out. Today, there are several different models of food dehydrators you can purchase. However, most of them rely upon electricity and therefore may not be very useful if the grid goes down.

Store the dehydrated foods in tight-sealing jars or zip-top baggies until you need them. If kept in a cool, dark place, dehydrated foods will last several months. Add the veggies to soups or stews, and they'll reconstitute nicely. Fruit can be eaten as is or added to pies.

FREEZE-DRYING

In just the last few years, the technology necessary for freeze-drying food has become at least somewhat accessible to the layperson. At the time of this writing, Harvest Right is the only company currently making freeze-dry units that are suitable for home use. While they are fairly expensive, if you're going to be preserving a lot of food on a regular basis, or if you have a large family or group that could go in together on the purchase, it might be worth exploring this option.

The differences between dehydrating and freeze-drying food are substantial, despite how similar the end results tend to appear. Freeze-drying preserves far more of the nutrient value in the food than dehydration. When you rehydrate food that's been dehydrated, the results can be less palatable than the freeze-dried versions.

Laurie Neverman has extensively documented her experiences with a freeze-dry unit at CommonSenseHome.com. I'd recommend checking it out before sinking money into purchasing one. She explains the good, the bad, and the ugly, so to speak.

SMOKING MEAT

Since ancient times, people have been preserving meat by smoking it. There are two types of smoking: hot and cold. Many people today are familiar with hot smoking, as it's the method used in the home smokers that are so popular. Hot smoking is a great way to make a brisket, but it won't do much at all for preserving the meat.

Instead, cold smoking is the way to go, and it doesn't require much in the way of equipment. Start by cobbling together some sort of rack or hanging system from which to suspend your meat. One possibility is to use those folding wooden racks designed to dry clothing in apartments. Another would be to use stakes and clothesline, though you need to be sure the weight of the meat won't cause the rope to dip too close to the ground or the fire.

Dig a small pit and build a fire in it. Use only hardwoods. Using softwoods like pine will give the meat a bad taste. For added flavor, use apple or hickory if available. You don't want a large, roaring fire either. You're after smoke, not heat. In fact, once the fire is burning well, soak some of the wood in water before adding it to the flames.

As the fire begins to burn, slice your meat into strips about an inch thick. Hang it from your rack, making sure no piece of meat is touching another. Enclose the fire and meat rack with a tarp, making sure the covering isn't close enough to burn or melt from the fire. Periodically check the fire and add fuel as needed. Having an oven thermometer handy will help you keep the temperature in the sweet spot of about 150°F to 155°F.

The meat is done when it is shriveled, dark, and brittle. Smoking for a day will keep the meat viable for about a week. If you can keep up the smoking for two full days, that will extend the preservation to a couple weeks to a month.

HOME CANNING

Home canning is the tried and true method of food preservation. Many of us have grandparents or great-grandparents who canned food as a matter of course. While it isn't a difficult skill, it does require an investment in supplies as well as time to learn properly.

There are two types of canning: water bath and pressure.

The water bath method consists of simply placing sealed jars of food on a rack and immersing them in boiling water for a set period of time. When the jars are removed from the water and cool down, the lids form a vacuum seal. This method is suitable only for acidic foods like fruits, preserves, and pickled vegetables. Anything else must be pressure canned.

Pressure canning involves the use of a—wait for it—pressure canner. Food is packed into jars and subjected to high pressure. This pressure causes the food to heat at much higher temperatures than it would in boiling water, killing botulism spores and other potential nasties.

Now, operating a pressure canner over an open flame is a bit trickier than doing so on a stove top, where you can more easily regulate the temperature. But it certainly can be done, and has been done for many years. It just takes a bit of practice.

If you want to pursue this method of food preservation, you'll need a pressure canner, plenty of jars and lids (I recommend the Tattler brand lids as they're reusable, but be sure to read and follow the instructions), a couple jar racks, and, above all, a good book detailing the exact process times for a wide range of foods. One of the best resources out there remains the *Ball Complete Book of Home Preserving*, edited by Judi Kingry and Laura Devine (Toronto, Canada: Robert Rose, 2006).

ROOT CELLARS

Provided you have the space for one, root cellars are another age-old method of preserving food. Essentially a hole in the ground, a root cellar stays a constant temperature and humidity year-round, providing a very stable environment in which to store food. While traditionally root cellars were used to store things like potatoes and turnips, you can realistically store just about any fruits or vegetables, with the possible exception of apples. Those give off ethylene gas, which causes other fruits to ripen quicker.

A rather easy way to make a small root cellar is to use a metal trash can with a lid. You want to locate it near your house so you don't have to trek a long distance to get to it. Avoid putting it in a low spot in the yard, where water is likely to collect in a heavy rain. Find a small rise in the terrain and dig a hole deep enough to bury the can, leaving the last few inches of it exposed. Put in your goodies, then put the lid on the can. Toss several inches of hay on top of the lid, then cover it with a tarp to help keep rain off. Weigh down the edges of the tarp so it doesn't blow away.

Every time you remove veggies from the root cellar, take a peek at what you're leaving for later use. Remove anything that is beginning to rot or mold. Toss that stuff on the compost pile.

The viable storage time for cellared fruits and vegetables varies considerably. Carrots can last up to six months, while broccoli will stay decent only for a week or two.

If you are thinking of adding a root cellar to your overall preps, I highly recommend consulting *Root Cellaring: Natural Cold Storage of Fruits Vegetables* by Mike and Nancy Bubel.

Incidentally, dirt is a great barrier against disease and such. When you harvest your crops, leave the dirt on them until you are ready to prepare them to eat.

FREEZING

For those who live in areas that have a real winter, with freezing temperatures, snow, and all that other fun stuff, you can obviously keep food frozen outside. I suggest putting it into a cooler or other container and placing something heavy on top to keep critters out.

In bear country, always keep any food stored outside suspended from a rope, high enough to where a bear can't reach.

I also suggest that if you have large pieces of meat, such as from a harvested deer, butcher it completely before storing it outside. This way, you already have the cuts made, and you aren't having to hack off frozen chunks of meat from the carcass, then thawing them to cook.

COOKING METHODS

When the power is out, you might need to get a little creative with meal preparation. This is truly an area to seek the experience and practice before the skills become necessary. Fortunately, the cook trying to put together a decent meal for the family has some great options.

In this section, we're not so much concerned with *what* we're cooking as we are with *how* we're going to cook it. Remember that prepping is about giving yourself options. Don't rely on just one method of cooking. Experiment with some or all of these ways to cook and see which ones work best for you.

PATIO GRILLS

If you have fuel for one, a patio grill is a truly viable option for off-grid cooking. One standard propane tank will last a while, provided you're not wasteful with it. Even a standard kettle-type charcoal grill works great, and when you run out of bags of charcoal, you can use dry branches and such instead.

Similarly, a wise investment would be one of those small patio fire pits that have become commonplace in the last few years. Take an old grill

INDOOR COOKING OPTIONS

The primary dangers with cooking indoors are carbon monoxide and fire. Any of the solid or gas fuel options discussed can be used indoors, provided you ensure there is decent ventilation. Simply cracking a window near where you're cooking will suffice. Anything involving burning charcoal or biomass should only be done outdoors.

Any type of cooking that involves a flame necessitates great care to ensure you don't burn the joint to the ground.

grate (found at a rummage sale if you don't have one lying around) and lay it across the top of the fire pit to provide a stable cooking surface.

CAMP STOVES

Hikers and campers have long used small portable stoves to heat water and food. These stoves fall into four categories, based on the type of fuel they use.

SOLID FUEL

The classic solid fuel stove is the Esbit Folding Pocket Stove. It uses fuel tablets that burn for about twelve minutes. One fuel tablet will bring 2 cups of water to a rolling boil. These work great for heating water for coffee or for rehydrating camp food, but using this type of stove to cook an entire meal for a family would be impractical.

PRESSURIZED GAS

Popular among hikers and backpackers, this type of stove uses a canister of pressurized gas and a mix of propane and butane, or iso-butane, for fuel. The stove itself is very small and functions as both burner and pot stand. The canister sits upright and the stove attaches to the top. As with the solid fuel stoves, this just isn't a viable option for long-term use unless you somehow have a source for hundreds of fuel canisters. One 4-ounce canister will typically last two people a couple of days when backpacking. Also worth noting, canister stoves can be rather finicky in cold weather.

LIQUID GAS

Liquid gas stoves use white gas, also known as naphtha. While the fuel is pressurized when in use, you create the pressure yourself via a pump system. This largely alleviates the problem with cold weather use that is common with the canister stoves. Liquid gas stoves are a little more complicated than their canister stove cousins, though. The fuel must be pressurized via pumping and the stove needs to be preheated. This isn't insurmountable, of course, but there is a distinct learning curve.

Stoves marketed as multi-fuel are liquid gas models that can use other fuels in addition to white gas, including kerosene, unleaded gasoline, and diesel. This expands your options quite a bit but in a long-term scenario, odds are that any available gasoline or diesel will be relegated to vehicle use only.

Related to this category are alcohol stoves. Unlike the others, alcohol isn't put under pressure before the stove is lit. You simply pour the fuel into the stove and light a match. There are innumerable websites and videos online describing how to make an alcohol stove out of a soda can. While fun, this isn't a great option for cooking dinner for the family.

BIOMASS

For the purposes of our discussion, biomass refers to things like sticks, twigs, and pine cones. Basically, dry natural material that will burn easily. In many parts of the world, you can find this fuel in abundance, which makes this the preferred type of camp stove for long-term use. The advantage this type of stove has over a campfire is efficiency. A

STERNO

You see Sterno used in restaurant buffet lines a lot. They are little cans of gel fuel that burn with a blue flame and keep the food hot. While they can and will cook food, it can be a time-consuming process. It is one thing if you're heating water for tea or warming up a can of stew. It is another thing entirely if you're trying to brown meat.

That said, Sterno doesn't require any sort of fancy stove. Bring in two or three small bricks or softball-sized rocks and put the can of Sterno between them, then rest your cook pot or tea kettle on the rocks.

relatively small amount of fuel can be used to heat water or cook food because the heat energy is contained and focused on the cooking vessel.

These stoves aren't very large, though, as they are intended to be packed and carried from campsite to campsite. As a result, they are fairly limited to what you can cook on them, at least in terms of quantity. As with any type of open-flame cooking, it takes experience and practice to get the hang of it.

CARDBOARD BOX OVEN

The supplies needed for this method should be readily available, either from your own storage or through a little scrounging. Many scouts have probably made a similar contraption at some point so for them, this will be a refresher. You might go so far as to build this oven while the materials are easy to find, play with it a few times, then store it away for future use.

You'll need:

- cardboard box or Bankers Box
- heavy-duty aluminum foil
- duct tape
- aluminum foil baking pan
- charcoal briquettes
- four empty soda cans, rocks, or small bricks
- small grill grate or large foil pan

An empty copy paper box is the perfect size for this project. If you can't find one, look for a banker box about the same size. Those can be purchased at any office supply store. However, if you're going there, you might ask them if they have one or two empty copy paper boxes they could toss your way. Never hurts to ask.

Line the interior of the box with foil, shiny side out. Overlap the foil to the outside of the box several inches and tape it down. Do not, however, use any tape inside the box. Duct tape burns, and you don't want to set fire to your oven. If you're struggling to get the foil to stay in place inside the box, you could use high-temperature flue tape or something similar. But, the foil should be rigid enough to stay in place by itself. Just make sure you cover the entire interior surface of the box.

Place the foil baking pan on a heat-resistant surface, such as on a flat area of bare ground or perhaps a large paver brick. Pour in the charcoal briquettes and light them up. How many briquettes depends on the temperature you want to achieve in the oven. Figure roughly 40°F per briquette. In my experience, nine briquettes is equal to about 350°F. Adjust the amount up or down to hit your approximate temperature target. As with most off-grid cooking methods, exact temperatures are difficult if not impossible to maintain. Use a chimney charcoal starter rather than lighter fluid to get the briquettes going. While a charcoal grill allows the smell of the lighter fluid to dissipate with the breeze, the fumes would become trapped in this oven and may lend an off taste to the food.

Fill the soda cans with a few inches of sand or dirt to weigh them down. Place the cans at the corners of the foil pan and use them to hold the grill grate above the briquettes. If you don't have cans readily available, use rocks or small bricks. The idea is to build a shelf above the briquettes. If you can't find a small enough grill grate, you can use a large foil pan, like you might use for a casserole or lasagna you're bringing to the church potluck.

Place the foil lined box upside down over the whole works and prop one end up about an inch or so with a small rock. This is for ventilation. Without it, the briquettes will stop burning. As it heats up, prepare your food, such as a cake or brownie mix.

Put the food on the grill grate and set your timer. Odds are, when you can smell the food, it'll be about done baking. It is important to fight the urge to peek on the food repeatedly. Lifting the box allows all the hot air to escape and thus results in a much longer cooking time.

COOKING TRIPOD

One essential tool for campfire cooking is a tripod. You can buy one at just about any camping or sporting goods store. They come with a grill grate that hangs from chains and you can easily raise or lower the grate by adjusting the chains. A tripod will fold up to store in the garage or shed until needed.

You can make one rather than buying it, of course. Find three straight branches about 6 or 7 feet long. They should be sturdy, about 2 inches thick. If you're in an urban area, branches might be scarce so hunt down a few closet rods about the right length. Closet rods are made to support weight, so they need not be as thick.

Hold the rods or branches together at one end and tie them together about a foot from the end. Spread the legs out into a triangle shape. Take a chain or rope and run it over the top of the tripod and down to the bail on the cookpot. Tie the other end of the rope to one of the legs to keep the cookpot in place.

Provided you handle it with care, the oven can be reused several times. If you run out of charcoal, you can use hot ashes and embers from a campfire, but you'll need to experiment to hit the right interior temperature. One tool that might be worth picking up is a candy thermometer. Shove the spike through the side of the box so the dial remains outside the box and thus visible.

CAMPFIRE COOKING

Cooking over a campfire involves just as much art as skill. The learning curve isn't particularly steep, but be prepared to end up with at least a few charbroiled briquettes at dinner until you've mastered the basics. Thus, it is highly advised you get a handle on this skill set now, rather than waiting until you have family members counting on you for their vittles.

What seems to be the most difficult aspect of campfire cooking for many people is the variable temperatures. This is why those in the know cook over the coals, not the flames. The heat is far steadier, though it is often higher than you might use on your stove.

There are a few different ways to approach cooking with a campfire. One of the easiest is to build what is called a keyhole fire. This is a campfire setup that is shaped, well, like a keyhole. Think of a traditional campfire with a ring of rocks around it. The keyhole setup adds a small kick out to one side of that circle. In other words, a circle with a rectangle jutting from one side.

For the keyhole fire, build the fire as you would normally in the main part of the campfire setup. Once you have a good supply of glowing coals, rake them into the kick-out area and cook over them. Add more coals as needed.

Many homes these days have some sort of fire pit on the back deck or patio. These work very well for campfire cooking. Quite a few of them come equipped with a grill grate, too. Again, though, cooking over coals is far easier than cooking over climbing flames.

PIT COOKING

People have been digging holes in the ground and cooking food in them for thousands of years. Earth is an excellent insulator. Basically, pit cooking amounts to heating up a hole in the dirt, putting food inside, and burying it for a while. There are two types of pit cooking: baking or steaming. For the most part, they are identical in terms of the basic process.

This is not a cooking method that you'd use for, say, heating up a can of soup. This is a type of cooking best suited for things like roasting chicken or fish. You could use pit cooking for making stew from scratch, too, if you have a container that seals well, such as a Dutch oven.

As one would guess, it starts by digging a pit. Contrary to what you might see on vacation in Hawaii, the pit need not be large enough to park a Volkswagen inside. While the size of the pit will depend on what you're planning to cook in it, figure about 2 square feet about 12 to 18 inches deep. Don't cart the dirt away, either. You'll need it later.

The pit needs to be lined with rocks, the flatter the better. Do not gather them from stream beds or other wet areas. They might have moisture inside that, when the rock is heated, will turn to steam and the rock may then explode, which will certainly ruin dinner. Line the bottom and all sides of the pit with the rocks. If you have a limited number of flattish rocks, use them for the bottom to provide as level of a surface as you can.

Build a fire in the pit to heat the rocks. The fire should be large enough to cover most of the pit's bottom. Keep adding fuel until the fire has burned for about an hour, then let it die down to coals. Keep the coals spread out on the bottom of the pit while you get the food ready to cook.

Now, this is where you must decide whether to bake or steam. If you're baking, skip this paragraph. If you're steaming, add a layer of seaweed or any edible green plants to the bottom of the pit, right on top of the coals. These will provide the moisture for steaming. You may go so far as to add a cup of water to the greens. You don't even need a cooking container. Assuming you're cooking something other than soup or stew, you can place the food directly on the plant material, then cover with another layer of greens. This works especially well with fish.

If you're baking, scrape the coals to one side of the pit. You could place your chicken or other food directly on the hot rocks if you lack a proper cooking vessel. Typically, the food is first wrapped in large leaves, though again these must be from a plant you know to be safe to eat. The leaves or the cooking vessel help prevent burning.

Once the food is in the pit, cover the hole with a piece of plywood, a rug, or some other material, then add a few inches of dirt on top. When steaming, some people use a piece of plastic and weigh it down on all sides to keep it in place. The plastic may swell a bit as steam builds inside the pit.

The cooking time will vary, of course, based on a number of factors, including what you're cooking. Figure roughly three hours as a standard and then experiment from there. When you think the food is done, simply dig it up.

WONDER OVEN

There is indeed an actual product called the Wonder Oven, thus the capitalization. The Wonder Oven is one of those ideas that is so old it is new again. The principles at work here have been in use for hundreds of years. The Wonder Oven is merely a modern version of what used to be called a hay box cooker. The idea is to bring the food up to a certain temperature, then place it into an insulated container and let it cook for a few hours. Think Crock Pot, without the electricity.

Back in the day, you'd build a box out of wood and fill it with hay. The pot of stew would be brought to a boil, covered, and buried in the hay. A lid placed on the box kept everything insulated well. The cook would set this up in the morning after breakfast and by dinner the stew would be ready to serve.

The modern Wonder Oven is sort of a large pillow filled with polystyrene beads. When the pot of food is wrapped up, the beads form something akin to a wall of Styrofoam around all sides, keeping the food hot for hours. Worth noting is that this will work just as well with cold food and drinks, acting as a cooler.

You can purchase a Wonder Oven online, premade and ready to go. There are also patterns you can purchase that allow you to sew your own, if you're handy with needle and thread. The polystyrene beads come in different sizes. Look for the 3-millimeter size as that seems to work the best. These are the same kind of beads that you'll find in a bean bag chair, though a bit smaller.

Now, all of that said, you can accomplish the same thing with a simple Styrofoam cooler and some blankets or towels. All you're doing is bringing the food up to cooking temperature, then insulating it while it cooks. What this does is conserve your fuel so you're not burning gas, wood, or other fuel source until the food is done cooking.

A few pointers on this method of cooking.

- The less air space in the cook pot, the better. Fill the pot as close to the top as possible.
- The lid should fit tightly. This isn't pressure cooking; it doesn't need to be strapped down. But there shouldn't be gaps between the lid and the pot.
- Meat should be browned first.
- Several folks have reported that thin-walled metal containers work best for Wonder Oven cooking. So, in this case, you can forgo the cast iron and use the cheaper stuff.

HOT STONE COOKING

A flat rock placed near a campfire will absorb heat and can then be used as a grill of sorts. There are a couple of ways to do this. The first is to suspend the flat rock over the fire by propping it up on legs made of smaller rocks. The other method is to heat the rock next to the fire for a while, then move it to the side and cook on it. Either way works well.

Select a flat rock that is 1 or 2 inches thick and large enough to hold whatever it is you want to cook. Avoid rocks that have cracks, and don't gather them from stream beds or other wet areas where the rock may have absorbed water. Scrub any dirt or debris from the rock before using it. Once the rock is hot, place the food directly on it for grilling.

While meats are the primary type of food cooked with this method, with steaks or fish just slapped right on the hot rock, anything that you'd normally cook on your patio grill can be cooked with a hot flat rock. Sliced pineapple, fresh or canned, is quite a treat when grilled.

When the rock has cooled, use a small amount of water to scrub it clean of any lingering bits of food and grease.

SOLAR OVEN

Another option to consider is building a solar oven. This is a device that is easily crafted at home from basic materials. It works well, but it isn't a very fast way to prepare a meal. It is also very weather contingent— rainy days don't make for very good cooking with a solar oven.

At the core, a solar oven is nothing more than an insulated box with a clear lid. Here are the basics on how to construct one:

You'll need two cardboard boxes, one a bit smaller than the other. As you choose your box sizes, bear in mind the smaller of the two is where you'll be putting your food. So, you'll want it at least large enough to fit a small pot or pan inside. Use flat black spray paint or black construction paper to completely cover the interior of the smaller box. Center that box inside the larger one and fill the space between the two with crumpled newspaper or shredded paper as an insulator. Cut off the box lid flaps on the smaller box, making the cuts as straight as possible.

Next, you need to find a clear lid. What works very well, provided you can find one of suitable size for your box, is the glass from an old photo frame. You want it large enough to cover the smaller box opening completely. If you can't find the right size of glass, you can head to your local hardware store and pick up a small sheet of clear plastic like Lexan and cut it down to size. Ideally, there should be little to no space between the top edges of the smaller box and the clear lid to trap as much air as possible. That's why when you cut the flaps, the edges should be as straight as you can manage.

Line the inside of the flaps of the larger box's lid with aluminum foil, gluing it down and smoothing out the wrinkles as best you can. What works well is to use a squeegee or ruler and run it along the foil, pressing firmly to iron it out.

Take the entire box oven out into the yard and find a sunny spot. Prop up the foiled flaps to reflect the sunlight into the box. Put your food on a dark-colored pie plate and place it in the box. Put the lid in place and let it sit. Check it regularly and turn the box as needed to keep the sun shining into it. You might also want to stir or reposition the food. Expect cooking temperatures of around 200°F, perhaps a bit more on a very sunny day, maybe as high as 350°F. The best times for using the solar oven will be from around 11:00 a.m. to 3:00 p.m. as that is when the sunlight will be strongest in most places.

COOKWARE

Most of your day-to-day pots and pans aren't designed for use over hot coals. Plastic handles will melt, for example, and thin aluminum pans will warp. Even higher-end stainless steel pans aren't made to be used over a campfire repeatedly. I *highly* suggest you pick up at least a few cast-iron skillets as well as a Dutch oven. Properly seasoned and maintained, they will last a lifetime or more of everyday use.

One of the best ways to season cast-iron cookware, although this method might not be feasible after a disaster, is to take the clean skillet and coat it with a thin layer of vegetable oil. Put it upside down in a 350°F oven for an hour, then turn the heat off and let it cool in the oven back to room temperature, which will take several hours. You might want to put a foil-covered cookie sheet on the rack underneath to catch drips as it cures. When cool, use a towel to wipe it down. If an oven isn't available, coat the cast-iron pan with oil, then set it right into the middle of a campfire for an hour, pull it out, and let it cool down.

Cast-iron cookware can be found at most department stores, but if you hunt around, you'll likely find bargains at thrift stores and rummage sales. If you find a pan that is rusty, you can scrub it out with either oil and coarse salt or with steel wool, then season it as outlined above.

To clean cast iron after use, just use a small amount of hot water and a nylon brush. Apply another thin coat of oil and you're good to go. If the pan has a lid, store it separately or at least put a paper towel or something between the lid and pan so air can get inside. When cooking with cast iron, keep in mind that the handle will be just about as hot as the rest of the pan. Therefore, always use a pot holder or thick towel to pick it up. One of the great things about cast iron is heat retention. The pan will stay hot for quite a while after being removed from the fire. You may want to leave a towel draped on the handle after you put the pan on the table or counter so you don't forget, grab the bare handle, and let loose with a string of expletives that would make a dock worker blush.

CHAPTER 4

MEDICINE: THERE'S A DOCTOR IN ALL OF US

One of the biggest challenges we've had to face is the lack of professional health care. I mean, we don't even have access to WebMD to self-diagnose! Fortunately, the police acted quickly enough and were able to protect the pharmacy in town. That's been quite a godsend to many of us. One of the three pharmacists who worked there lives here in town and has been working double shifts trying to keep up with demand. We also have a few experienced nurses and even a dental technician, but no doctors, no surgeons, no dentists. The EMTs we have are great with patching up cuts and scrapes, but all of their training has been concentrated on stabilizing a patient to get them to a hospital for treatment, not so much on actual long-term medical care.

We had a pretty severe flu outbreak about a month ago. They were doling out various over-the-counter meds to those who needed help with symptoms of vomiting, diarrhea, and such. Not much they could do about fighting the actual bug. I'll tell you, the stomach flu is infinitely worse when indoor plumbing isn't an option anymore.

As might have been expected, the first few weeks of the crisis brought a lot of injuries as people tried to figure out how to properly use things like chainsaws and hand tools. While no one lost a leg, as far as I've heard, there were a couple fingers lopped off, several heart attacks, and quite a few infections that resulted from cuts and punctures not being treated properly.

Dental issues have also been cropping up a fair amount. Several people had been fighting off various and sundry cavities and mouth infections even before the crisis hit. They are doing the best they can down at the new makeshift clinic, but antibiotics are being used only in the most severe cases. Once our supply of those meds is gone, we have no way to get more, so we're rationing it out based on priority.

Just about everyone who was on lifesaving medications, like heart meds or even insulin, is gone now. There are a few who are lingering, but I don't think they'll last much longer.

One of the most critical elements of any long-term survival plan is to account for medical needs. This goes beyond that small first aid kit you keep in your glove box. That will work great for small cuts and scrapes, but the longer a crisis goes on, the more likely it is that people are going to need help with more serious injuries and illnesses.

Like any other aspect of postcollapse life, you are going to be pretty much on your own when it comes to providing for your medical needs. While we would all love to have a couple of MDs within our survival group, that likely won't happen for most of us. And while we might dream of having a fully stocked emergency room at our fingertips, odds are pretty good that any in the area will have long since been looted and picked clean.

MEDICAL TRAINING

All the supplies on the planet won't do you much good if you don't know how to use them properly. I'm not saying you need to go out and enroll in medical school tomorrow morning (though if that's a feasible option for you, please feel free). However, there are a few different avenues worth exploring to increase your medical knowledge and skills.

Many technical colleges offer courses of interest within their emergency medical technician (EMT) programs. Even if you have no plans to

DISCLAIMER: I AM NOT A DOCTOR

Nor have I ever played one on television. The information provided in this chapter is based upon research as well as my own experience. Nothing here should ever replace the advice and treatment received from a competent medical professional. If a long-term crisis were to come to pass, make every effort to seek out medical care before resorting to extreme measures on your own.å pursue that career path, the training and knowledge will be very useful. If you lack the funds to pay the tuition, look into auditing the classes. Some schools allow students to attend certain classes, even take the exams, without receiving an actual grade, certificate of completion, or credit toward a degree. Typically, this is done in exchange for a reduced class fee. For our purposes, getting the knowledge is more important than getting a piece of paper certifying you were there.

If it is a large school, you might even be able to just sneak into class and observe, soaking in the information unobtrusively. When I was in college, we did this from time to time to get a feel for whether we'd like a certain professor or class. Granted, that was at a fairly large university, where one more face in a crowd of several hundred wasn't too obvious. Your mileage, as they say, may vary.

Even basic first aid training through the Red Cross or another similar agency will teach you how to properly treat a wound, set a broken limb, and other valuable skills. Do yourself a favor and seek out this training at every opportunity.

MEDICAL TEXTS

While medical training is something that should ideally be gained through hands-on, or at least face-to-face, experience, you can pick up a fair amount simply through studying various books. Even if you have extensive training, it is a good idea to put together a medical library of sorts. Bear in mind, though, the importance of actually reading these books, rather than just sticking them on a shelf in case you need them someday. It is only through reading and studying the texts that you'll not only learn skills to treat illness and injury but know which books are best to consult in certain circumstances.

Here are some books in my own medical library:

US Army Special Forces Medical Handbook
by Glen C. Craig (Boulder, CO: Paladin Press, 1988)

The Survival Medicine Handbook: A Guide for When Help Is Not on the Way, 4th edition
by Joseph and Amy Alton (Weston, FL: Doom and Bloom, 2021)

PDR for Herbal Medicines, 4th edition
by Thomson Healthcare (Montvale, NJ: Thomson Healthcare, Inc., 2007)

Where There Is No Doctor: A Village Health Care Handbook, 18th edition
by David Werner, Carol Thuman, and Jane Maxwell (Berkeley, CA: Hesperian Health Guides, 2022)

Where There Is No Dentist
by Murray Dickson (Berkeley, CA: Hesperian Health Guides, 2021)

Every year brings a new edition of the vaunted *Physician's Desk Reference*, also known as just *PDR*. This guide to prescription medications is a great source for determining what specific drugs are used for, which should not be used together, and other critical information. However, given the expected lack of prescription medications in a postcollapse world, this particular resource is perhaps secondary to the ones listed above.

I also have various and sundry textbooks for nursing programs and emergency medical tech courses. Most of those I've picked up for spare change at thrift stores. You can also purchase used books in these and other fields right at university and technical school bookstores, though they'll likely be on the pricey side. Shopping for specific titles online could save you a few bucks.

It is important to have actual hard copies of these books and manuals on hand. While e-books are often cheaper, and they certainly don't take up valuable shelf space, you can't count on that Kindle or other e-reader being accessible to you weeks or months after the crisis begins.

MEDICAL SUPPLIES

Of course, in addition to the training and texts, you'll need the tools with which to work. To better understand what might be needed, let's first talk about the most probable injuries and illnesses that will befall survivors.

Lacerations and contusions are going to be very common. Given that many, if not most, people are not used to working with their hands and engaging in manual labor for long periods of time, there is bound to be a learning curve. Along the way, cuts, abrasions, and bruising will occur with regularity. Any open wound, no matter how slight, needs to be bandaged to prevent infection. Today's healthiest adults still cannot compete with the immune systems of those who lived years ago. For better or worse, we live in something of a bubble today and generally aren't exposed to all the germs our forebears were. As a result of this rather sterilized existence, we fall prey to infections easier. Until our immune systems get back on track, so to speak, we need to provide as much assistance as we can.

TREATING A LACERATION

A laceration is a cut in the skin. As with punctures, this sort of injury will be rather common. Fortunately, the vast majority of lacerations are easily treated.

Allow the wound to bleed for a few minutes to clean it from the inside. Then, use direct pressure for several minutes to stop the bleeding.

Clean the wound and surrounding area with plain water. You want to avoid getting any sort of soap directly in the wound, so stick with just clean water.

Pat the wound dry and apply butterfly bandages, pulling the wound closed as you do so. Do not whip out the suture kit unless you absolutely know what you're doing. Keep the wound covered when there is a chance of dirt getting into it. Otherwise, keeping it exposed to open air will help speed healing.

Expect to see a fair number of sprains and strains. Again, people are going to be much more physically active than they may have been in the past, and their bodies won't be used to it. Cutting firewood, for example, for those who aren't accustomed to it, brings with it the possibility for lower-back and shoulder injuries, as well as those incurred from accidents.

Depending on how things shake out with your security plans, there is also the possibility of gunshot wounds. These are problematic at best, and bring with them the risk of life-threatening infection. Any sort of puncture wound causes germs and bacteria from the surface of your skin to be driven into the body.

When you have a group of diverse people living in close quarters for long periods of time, you may see infestations of lice and such crop up. All it takes is for one person to have a few nits at the beginning of the crisis and, within days, the entire group is itching and scratching. Do everyone a favor and stock up on the appropriate remedies.

You can also expect to see burn injuries here and there due to the increased use of open flame for cooking as well as light. Hopefully, the majority of those burns will be minor. Those who do get singed will be thankful if you've stocked up on burn cream ahead of time.

As for illnesses, you'll see a number of instances of digestive problems as people's diets change. On top of that, as we're forced to resort to actual face-to-face communication rather than relying upon email and text messaging, we're going to be in contact with more viruses and diseases. Couple that with the fact that hygiene won't necessarily be high on many people's priority lists and you'll see contagious illnesses, from the common cold to the stomach flu, spreading quickly through any group.

Now that we have an idea of what to expect, let's look at some supplies to have on hand.

WOUND CARE

Take a look at your first aid supplies. How many boxes of bandages do you have? I'm betting it isn't nearly enough, to be honest with you. Think about it like this: Just a single serious injury, say an accidental knife cut along the forearm, will require regular changing of bandages. Say you change them three times a day, and it takes a good week for the wound to heal up enough that you can get by with simply covering it with a wrap. That's twenty-one bandages needed for just that one injury. If you are looking to provide for most or all of your family's medical needs for a year or more, those bandages could add up quickly.

One way to ease that challenge is to make your own dressings. Take old T-shirts and cut them into rectangles, say, twelve inches long and six inches high. You can probably get two or three rectangles from an average T-shirt. Wash them in hot water with lots of bleach, then boil them for several minutes. They might shrink up a bit if they are 100 percent cotton, but that's OK. Take these homemade dressings and store them in plastic bags. If you're feeling particularly ambitious, you could vacuum seal them if you have such a device.

Even with those precautions, I don't know that you could consider those dressings completely sterile. But, once the wound has closed, you can use these fabric scraps rather than store-bought bandages. This will extend your supplies a bit.

Don't shortchange yourself on butterfly bandages. These will be used to keep large wounds closed. It is difficult, if not almost impossible, to improvise this sort of bandage, so be sure to have a large quantity available.

Hemostatic bandages, such as those found under the brand name QuikClot, work extremely well in controlling bleeding. They aren't cheap but will be worth their weight in gold in the event of a traumatic injury.

As I've mentioned more than once, the risk of infection needs to be addressed with any wound. When feasible, apply an antibiotic ointment, such as Neosporin. If it isn't available, using simple petroleum jelly will be beneficial. The idea is to keep nasties from getting into the wound.

Along those same lines, invest in several bottles of hydrogen peroxide and rubbing alcohol. Both will be useful in cleaning wounds, though hydrogen peroxide is the far less painful of the two.

TREATING A PUNCTURE WOUND

Puncture wounds may prove to be somewhat common, given the work that will be done to clear debris resulting from a disaster. There is always a danger of infection with any wound, and this is especially true for punctures. The nail or object that caused the wound will drive any germs or bacteria on the surface of the skin deep into the body. Therefore, it is crucial you do all you can to clean the wound properly.

When presented with a puncture wound, first verify whether the foreign object has been removed. If possible, examine the object to see if perhaps a small piece may have broken off inside the body. Let the wound bleed for a few minutes, unless there is an immediate danger of extreme blood loss. The blood coming from the wound helps to clean it from the inside out. After a few minutes, stop the bleeding using direct pressure on the wound.

If you believe any portion of the foreign object remains in the wound, use a clean pair of tweezers to try and remove it. No, this will not feel very good to the patient. It still needs to be done.

Clean the wound thoroughly with mild soap and lots of water. If you have it available, apply some antibiotic cream then cover the wound with a bandage. Replace the bandage daily or if it gets soiled. Watch for signs of infection, such as swelling, pus discharge, or spreading redness.

WRAPS AND SPLINTS

As an injured limb heals, it is important to keep it immobilized. This is where elastic wraps and splints come into play. One reason you want to use elastic rather than just wrapping the ankle with layers of old shirts is the elastic (if applied properly) won't restrict circulation. Proper circulation will help the injury heal. Plus, restricting the blood flow could cause additional harm to the extremity. Honestly, elastic wraps are so inexpensive, it is foolish to not stock up.

Splints are another thing that you could conceivably improvise as necessary. Popsicle sticks work well for fingers, as an example. When feasible, consider padding the splint with cloth for the patient's comfort.

PURCHASED FIRST AID KITS VS. DIY KITS

There are some pretty great first aid kits out there for purchase…and a whole lot of kits that aren't worth squat. Most of the ones you'll find at department stores and discount retailers aren't designed for much more than a few bumps and bruises suffered at a child's soccer game. Plus, if you take a hard look at the content lists of those kits and do the math, you aren't saving all that much money over buying the components separately.

What is a workable option is to purchase a commercial first aid kit as a base, but then add to it. Any first aid kit you buy will need to be tailored to your specific situation. Add in any components that are applicable to you and your family, such as prescription medications. If anyone is allergic to certain things, such as bee stings, be darn sure you have plenty of epinephrine and such available.

I recommend that you set up one location in your home, say a couple shelves in a bathroom closet, to use as your primary first aid gear stash. This is where you'll store extra boxes of bandages, bottles of hydrogen peroxide, and other bulk items. On one of the shelves or perhaps on the floor of the closet, keep a kit that is comprehensive yet portable. Some folks like to use giant rolling tackle boxes, for example. Others prefer a soft-sided duffle bag. The point is to have at least one kit that has some of everything in it, yet is portable enough that you can grab it and take it to where the injured party is located. Call this kit your "crash bag" and make sure everyone in the family knows what it is and where it is located. In an emergency, if you holler to someone to bring you the crash bag, the last thing you want to see is a confused expression on their face. As you use up the items in the crash bag, replenish them with your stockpiled supplies.

THE PREPPER'S MEDICINE CABINET

Pain relievers and fever reducers
- ibuprofen
- ibuprofen
- acetaminophen
- naproxen
- aspirin

Stomach upset
- Pepto-Bismol
- Imodium
- antacids

Cough and cold remedies
- cough syrup
- throat lozenges
- NyQuil
- DayQuil
- vitamin C lozenges or drops

Prescription medications
- thirty-day supply (minimum) of any necessary meds

Note: If you have children, make sure you have age-appropriate medications for them as well.

MEDICATIONS

In addition to the bandages and other first aid supplies, you'll need different types of medications on hand. The problem is that meds— unlike elastic wrap, for example—have a shelf life. While most of them won't harm you if taken past their "best by" date, they lose effectiveness over time. Medications, like food, need to be rotated so they are always fresh. Luckily, most over-the-counter meds have shelf lives of a year or more, so you won't need to replenish your stock every few months.

PAIN RELIEVERS AND FEVER REDUCERS

This is the category of medications you will likely turn to the most. Few people truly enjoy being in any degree of pain. And while pain is the body's way of communicating to the brain that something is amiss, once that message is received and understood, the brain wants the body to shut the hell up about it.

Fever is one of the body's defense mechanisms, an attempt to "burn out" the infection or illness. That being the case, I often eschew medicating against a fever, unless it gets very high or prolonged. All other things being equal, why not let your body do the work?

Ibuprofen, acetaminophen, and aspirin top the list of common pain relievers. Of these, I personally turn to ibuprofen for most aches and pains. For reducing fever, I prefer acetaminophen. Aspirin, for all its benefits, can cause stomach upset more so than the other two. No matter which medications you decide to stock, it is important to understand proper dosages. Many people go overboard with pain relievers, taking far more than they truly should. This does little good and actually can be quite harmful in the long run.

If you have children, be sure to stock up on the child-safe versions of these medications. Having 500-mg acetaminophen tablets won't do you much good if your four-year-old can't take them when her fever crests at 102°F.

Recent studies show that regular-strength Tylenol can also help control general anxiety. Indications are that taking 1000-mg of acetaminophen can help lower emotional pain, particularly the pain stemming from anxiety.

COUGHS AND COLDS

During times of high stress, our immune systems are often negatively affected. As a result, we are more vulnerable to things like the flu or common cold. While over-the-counter medications don't do much to cure the ailment, they do treat the symptoms of coughs, sore throats, and nasal congestion, and are nice to have on hand.

STOMACH UPSET

As noted earlier, tummy troubles may be common, especially in the early days of a collapse. On top of the changes in diet and consuming questionable water, stomach upset is a common result of an increase in stress and anxiety. Bismuth subsalicylate, known commonly as Pepto-

ANTIBIOTICS

It has become common knowledge among preppers and survivalists that most veterinary antibiotics, such as "fish mox" (amoxicillin) are very similar or even identical to the medicines used by humans. Less clear is which medicines are used in which situations. Not to mention that many people rely on antibiotics to treat ailments and issues for which they'll do exactly nothing.

That said, antibiotics have saved countless lives and having them in the medicine cabinet isn't a bad idea, provided you do your homework. Start with a copy of *Alton's Antibiotics and Infectious Disease: The Layman's Guide to Available Antibacterials in Austere Settings* by Joseph Alton, MD, and Amy Alton, ARNP. This is the best layman's reference I've found on the subject.

As for legally obtaining antibiotics, you have a couple of options. Some pet stores and many farm stores sell veterinary medications, either at the store or online. There are countries outside the United States where you can purchase some antibiotics over the counter. One more approach is to utilize a company like JASE Medical (jasemedical.com). They offer an emergency pack of various antibiotics, though you'll need to go through a short online review process with their medical staff.

Bismol, is one of the most popular remedies for such issues. Available in a liquid as well as chewables and even tablets, there is no reason to not have a good quantity on hand. However, avoid giving it to children who are recovering from the flu or chicken pox, due to the risk of Reye's syndrome.

Antacids are also highly recommended. I've often found they are helpful with nausea as well as heartburn and acid reflux. That's not a doctor speaking, of course, just my own experience talking.

Loperamide (trade name: Imodium) is another medication that works well on diarrhea. However, it is not recommended for treating digestive upset that is the result of E. coli or salmonella.

PRESCRIPTION MEDICATIONS

This is a troublesome area for many people. Every year, more and more people are placed on prescription medications for a wide range of ailments, from heart disease to psychiatric issues. With many of these drugs, stopping cold turkey, whether intentionally or not, can be harmful. To add to the problem, while many doctors are amenable to providing patients with a backup supply of these medications (with the possible exception of narcotic pain relievers), insurance companies usually don't want to foot the bill.

My first suggestion is for you to talk with your prescribing physician. Explain your concern about stocking up on necessary medications in the event of an emergency that would prevent you from running to Walgreens. I would *not*, however, suggest you tell him or her that you are planning for a society-ending event. While I'm certain there are doctors out there who are just as concerned as we are about these sorts of things, unless you know your doctor is one of them, avoid that particular line of discussion.

If your insurance won't cover the cost of an extra supply of medications, see if you can afford to pay out of pocket for a month or two. While exorbitantly expensive, you might be able to swing it if you save up for a bit. Another option is to always refill your prescription as soon as you can rather than just when you're about to run out. By allowing the scripts to overlap a bit, you can set aside a day or two's worth of meds each month *without skipping a dose*. Always take the oldest medication first. Over time, you can build up at least a small supply.

When you speak with your doctor about this, ask him or her about what could happen if you aren't able to take the medication. If there are

WHAT ABOUT INSULIN?

Diabetes is the scourge of our society today. It seems like there are more diabetics in a single major city than existed across the entire country a few decades ago. Whether this is a result of our diets, our general lack of fitness, or something else, I have no idea. What I do know is that if the trucks stop delivering insulin to pharmacies, it won't be long before there are some serious ramifications.

If you or a loved one is an insulin-dependent diabetic, learn as much as you can about controlling the disease through diet and lifestyle changes. While this isn't a workable solution for all, it can have benefits for many. Some forms of insulin are very stable and can be stored in cool conditions for a year or more. Talk to your doctor or pharmacist about switching to one of those products if you are not using them already.

Of course, that raises the question of how you'd keep it cool in a grid-down environment, right? I know there's at least one line of products designed to do that very thing. The one I'm familiar with is manufactured and sold by a company called Frio. Their insulin-cooling wallets and carrying cases work via evaporation. You simply soak the cooler packs with plain water, and crystals inside turn to a gel. Evaporation is a cooling process, so as the gel dries out, it cools the inside of the case. Each soaking will provide almost two full days' worth of cooling effect, and you can repeat the process as needed.

Find them online at www.FrioInsulinCoolingCase.com.

withdrawal effects, what can you do about them? Are there over-the-counter meds that will help alleviate those problems?

MEDICAL EQUIPMENT

In addition to the basic stuff like meds and bandages, there are a few different tools and such that you will want to acquire.

Good old-fashioned thermometers will be necessary to accurately gauge a fever. Make sure you know the difference between an oral thermometer and a rectal one, using each appropriately. While there are all sorts of handy gadgets nowadays, such as battery-powered thermometers that check ear temperature or ones that you just swipe across the forehead, do yourself a favor and go the low-tech route. Also be sure to have at least a couple in case one gets lost or broken.

A blood pressure cuff is also great to have when monitoring a patient. Though not absolutely necessary in most cases, you may find yourself turning to it often if you have one.

A stethoscope allows you to check on lung and breathing concerns. Spring for a decent-quality one that is at least a few steps up from your kid's doctor play set.

Nitrile gloves are a necessity. The first rule of providing medical care is to protect yourself first. It will do no one any good if you render care only to end up getting sick yourself or—much worse—spreading a disease to others. Whenever humanly possible, glove up before touching a patient or cleaning up any of a patient's messes.

Surgical masks are another good thing to have along these same lines.

I often see suture kits and other surgical equipment recommended. I'm on the fence about them, myself. If you have the skills and knowledge to use such tools effectively, by all means have some on hand. However, if you don't know what you're doing, you will likely end up doing much more harm than good. If you are hell-bent on having these items, seek out the necessary training to use them properly.

DENTAL ISSUES

As someone who has suffered from hereditary tooth problems for a couple of decades now, I can say from practical experience that it is even less fun than you might imagine. The importance of dental health cannot be overstated. It can impact several other areas of your body, including your heart, and lead to a litany of problems if not handled properly.

First and foremost, seek professional, competent care whenever feasible. Don't let problems linger or fester. While you might be able to keep an infection under control with antibiotics, that's not going to take care of the root cause, and the infection is just likely to come back stronger at some point. If you do not have dental insurance, ask about some sort of payment plan or sliding scale for fees. Failing that, find out if there is a dental school within reasonable driving distance. If so, contact them, as they often have programs where students can treat patients, while being supervised by licensed dentists, of course.

You should have a good stockpile of lidocaine, which you can buy over the counter near the toothpaste and mouthwash. It is sold as a numbing agent for tooth or gum pain. In the same aisle, you'll find temporary tooth repair kits that have filling material for chips, cracks, and such. While not perfect, they're better than nothing. Pain relievers like ibuprofen will be beneficial as well.

As for extractions and other procedures, refer to *Where There Is No Dentist* by Murray Dickson (Berkeley, CA: Hesperian Health Guides, 2012). It will help guide you through various dental problems and how to handle them in austere settings, which is beyond the scope of our discussion here.

BIRTH CONTROL

While I fully realize some readers may feel this section belongs in the chapter on entertainment, we'll discuss it here instead.

The fact is, procreation is one of our strongest compulsions as a species. On top of that, it is not at all uncommon for people to turn to sexual activity as a way to alleviate stress and anxiety in the wake of an emergency situation. Not to mention, it is a fairly enjoyable way to pass the time when the power's out, right?

With all that in mind, I encourage you to stock up on a supply of birth control methods, such as condoms. Birthing a child in our modern society is generally a lot easier than it was in decades past. We enjoy a level of medical technology that allows for immediate action in the event of complications. Back in the day, not so much. In a postcollapse world, we won't have access to all those goodies and, as a result, pregnancy and childbirth could prove to be much more hazardous.

Yes, I know, women have been birthing babies since the dawn of humanity. An awful lot of them, though, didn't live to actually see their baby. A substantial number of babies never made it to their first birthday either.

Go through the motions of procreation all you want, just do what you can to minimize the number of pregnancies.

While we're on the subject, sexually transmitted diseases might become an issue at some point, depending, of course, on the configuration of your group. This is another reason to stock up on condoms, though bear in mind they only last a year or two before becoming fairly unusable.

NATURAL REMEDIES

Stockpiled medications aren't going to last forever. They will be used up or lose their effectiveness over time. For this reason alone, it is important to get a handle on ways to allow nature to help you treat your patients. The fact is, a high percentage of medications in use today were originally derived from plants and other natural sources. We have been more or less trained, maybe even indoctrinated, to believe the cure for all our ails lies within a prescription bottle. Yet nature is absolutely teeming with its own forms of medicine, most of which are actually healthier for us than the chemical concoctions prescribed to millions every day.

If we have a headache, we don't think twice about reaching for an aspirin. But many of us might scoff at the person drinking willow bark tea, despite the fact that the medicine being taken in either case is almost identical. For many, it might just be a matter of convenience. After all, we, as a society, want everything to be fast and easy, from our food to our entertainment. After a collapse, though, we might not have the luxury of simply popping a couple pills to fix a problem. I suggest you avail yourself of any and all local resources for learning more about natural remedies, and invest in at least a few guides for plant identification and use. Here are some books I'd particularly recommend:

A Field Guide to Medicinal Plants and Herbs: Eastern and Central North America (Peterson Field Guides), 3rd edition
by Steven Foster and James A. Duke (Boston, MA: Mariner Booksx, 2014). Note there is also an edition for the Western region.

Medicinal Plants of the Southern Appalachians
by Patricia Kyritsi Howell (Mountain City, GA: BotanoLogos, 2006)

Prepper's Natural Medicine: Lifesaving Herbs, Essential Oils, and Natural Remedies for When There Is No Doctor
by Cat Ellis (Berkeley, CA: Ulysses Press, 2015)

Nothing beats practical, hands-on experience, though. Talk to the people who work at natural foods stores and see if they can put you in touch with someone local who teaches herbal remedies and related topics. You could also try contacting someone at your local county extension office as they might know of an expert in your area. What you want is someone who can take you out into the fields and forests, and show you how to identify the helpful plants. Field guides are great, but plants obviously change their appearance through their life cycle. Having someone who can take you by the hand and guide you to the plants you seek is invaluable experience.

Something else to keep in mind with natural remedies is it isn't an exact science. For example, while we know that garlic has wonderful antibiotic properties, the use and dosage isn't always going to be exactly the same for each person and each situation. There is something of a "fudge factor" involved. Where prescription medications are produced to exacting standards, plants are not. The plantain that grows this year will not be identical to the plantain growing next year. Further, the effects these plants have on humans vary from person to person, at least a bit. What works great for one infection might not do so well on the next. Therefore, gaining experience with trial and error now, when times are good and you can afford to make mistakes, is recommended.

What follows are just a few of the more useful plants that are commonly found in most areas. Learn to identify these plants at all stages of their growth cycles. Perhaps even cultivate small crops of them so you'll always have them available to you.

Garlic works rather well as a natural antibiotic when consumed. You can also crush the cloves and add a bit of water to make a paste, then apply it as a poultice to fight infection. In this form, it will also provide relief to sore muscles and joints.

Aloe vera, as many of you already know, is great for treating burns, including sunburn. Cut or break off a piece and crush it to expose the thick sap. Apply the sap over the burn for rapid relief.

Crushed or chewed **plantain** is excellent for all sorts of rashes and itches. Used as a poultice, it will also help draw out toxins from a wound and help speed healing.

A tea made from **ginger** works very well at settling upset stomachs and helping with digestive issues.

Another tea, this one made from **pine needles**, provides an excellent source of vitamin C, which is known to augment the immune system.

Burdock is useful when treating problems on or just beneath the skin, such as abrasions, skin irritations, and burns. This is another plant that can be used as a poultice. Break up the leaves to expose the inner surface, then apply directly to the skin.

Yarrow is exceptional with bleeding wounds. Tear up the leaves a bit and apply to the wound. It will help speed clotting.

I cannot stress enough the importance of learning these and other natural remedies. In a long-term, grid-down situation, your only medicine cabinet might be the one outside the front door.

CHAPTER 5

HYGIENE: STAYING CLEAN IN A DIRTY WORLD

I feel like I'll never be truly clean again. I mean, we do what we can to wash up every day, but we all miss having a nice, hot shower or bath. Having someone dump a bucket of cold rainwater over your head just isn't the same. Plus, since indoor plumbing is now a thing of the past, none of us are relishing the thought of trying to bathe outside once the snow starts to fly.

We've been doing a lot of sponge baths, of course, out of necessity. Even after washing up, though, you still feel dirty.

There's no real polite way to say this—we all stink. What's interesting is the body odors aren't entirely unpleasant, actually. Everyone has sort of a unique scent, some stronger than others. Teenagers in particular; you can smell some of them coming a mile away. You'd think that after these last few months, the house would smell like a locker room. On hot days, it does get a bit ripe. But I am surprised at how little it bothers us. I guess we're just used to it.

Toothpaste is becoming a rather hot commodity in the neighborhood. Most of us have enough toothbrushes, at least for the time being, but toothpaste is running out in many homes. Between this and the body odor issues, many people tend to have their conversations at something of a distance.

There is some good news, though: We were checking for odds and ends in Uncle Craig's RV, which he'd parked here a few months before The Event. I don't see it as looting but rather rent for the storage space, ha ha. Anyway, we didn't find any food but did come across four whole rolls of toilet paper! Since there are four of us, we decided we'd each get one roll. That way, no one can be accused of using more than their fair share of this "jackpot."

I don't know which is sadder—that finding a few rolls of butt wipe made us feel like we'd won the lottery or that we actually raced each other to the latrine so we could partake in such luxury...

It is said that cleanliness is next to godliness. I don't know if that's true or not, but it is surely related to healthiness. While the absence of running water, not to mention the lack of a working water heater, can make washing up difficult, it is not impossible to keep reasonably clean in the wake of a collapse.

OFF-GRID TOILET FACILITIES

In a short-term emergency, toilets will still flush without running water. All you need to do is fill the tank with rainwater, and you're good to go (no pun intended). However, in a long-term situation, sewer lines are going to back up and the waste will have nowhere to go. Therefore, you need to plan ahead.

Chemical toilets, found in just about any camping store, will work, but they do require a stockpile of the chemicals they use to treat the waste. You may be better off with one of the following DIY solutions.

A five-gallon bucket can be fitted with a toilet seat. In fact, you can even buy seats that are specially made for this exact purpose. Fill the bucket with a few inches of sand. Keep another bucket of sand nearby, with a scoop in it. After doing your business, you scoop a bit of sand over the waste, maybe sprinkling some baking soda or powder laundry detergent in as well to help with odors. Once the bucket gets about half-full, you'll need to empty it before it gets too heavy to move easily.

A similar approach is to do away with the sand and just use heavy-duty garbage bags. Be sure to replace them while the bag is still easy to move. It would be considerably unpleasant to be lugging a giant bag of waste and have it break open.

Another solution, albeit involving a bit more work, is to dig a latrine. You'll want a trench that is at least a couple feet deep, about two feet wide, and several feet in length. To use, simply straddle the trench and do what you have to do. After each trip to the latrine, shovel a bit of dirt back over the waste. Locate the latrine at least a few hundred feet from any water source.

Few of us probably have the space to store a year or two's worth of toilet paper. If you do, feel free. For the rest of us, though, we'll need to figure out something else to use. Newsprint might work, as might old magazines. But my suggestion is to save up old shirts and socks. Rather than tossing them once they develop holes, cut them into squares about four or five inches on a side. Use these so-called "family cloths" in place of toilet paper. Keep a container in the bathroom, one with a tight-fitting lid, into which you can put the used cloths. They can be washed and reused many times, just like cloth diapers.

Plastic squeeze bottles are also handy to have in this regard. Often called a peri bottle, it is filled with water and the stream directed toward your bum. Think of it as a manual version of a bidet.

One of the most important things is to clean your hands after using the toilet. This cannot be stressed enough. One easy solution is to keep a bottle of hand sanitizer near the potty facilities. Prolonged use will tend to dry out the skin, so you may also want to have some sort of lotion available. Keep in mind it is alcohol in the sanitizer that allows it to evaporate quickly. Avoid putting your hands near an open flame right after using it. This includes lighting a smoke, lest you find out just how flammable alcohol fumes can be.

LAUNDRY

Doing laundry is another thing that, in a short-term situation, you might not need to worry much about. But, when we're planning for an event that could last weeks, months, or even longer, we're eventually going to run out of clean clothes. Unfortunately, doing laundry by hand is both time-consuming and exhausting. Do it once or twice and you'll see why the advent of the mechanical clothes-washing machine was such a blessing to households around the world. You'll also question the wisdom of wearing denim jeans all the time.

There are a few different ways to go about this. You could go old school and purchase a corrugated washboard and a large tub. Fill the tub with water, add detergent, and scrub away. Use a biodegradable laundry soap, such as Seventh Generation or Mountain Green. Rinse the clothes in another tub of water and hang them to dry.

You could even do without the washboard. Fill a bucket with soapy water and soak the clothes for a bit. Then, slap them against a large rock, scrubbing out the more stubborn stains, then rinse and hang.

The third method, and perhaps the easiest on your back and arms, is to build a washing machine of sorts out of a pail. Start with a five-gallon bucket that has a matching lid. You'll also need a clean toilet plunger, the old-fashioned rubber kind. Cut a hole in the top of the lid, right in the center, just big enough to accommodate the plunger handle. Then, using a sharp knife or razor, cut three or four half-dollar size holes in the rubber end of the plunger. Space the holes evenly apart.

Fill the bucket about halfway with water and add soap. Toss in a few shirts or a pair of pants, put in the plunger, and thread the lid over the plunger handle. Use the plunger to agitate the clothes up and down and side to side for a few minutes. No need to go at this like you're churning butter, just steady motions will do the trick. The lid is there to help prevent water from splashing everywhere, but you should still expect to get a little wet through all this.

Keep a small scrub brush nearby and use that to help remove ground-in dirt. Once the clothes are clean (or as clean as they're going to get), wring them out into the bucket, then rinse them in another one and hang to dry.

Obviously, whichever method you use, laundry is something that will likely take the better part of an entire day if you're washing clothes for the family. But this is also a chore that can be delegated rather easily to children.

Don't forget to recycle the water by reusing it in the gardens or even for bathing. This is why I suggested you use a biodegradable detergent, free of harsh chemicals that could harm you or your plants.

BATHING

For general bathing, a very workable solution is to purchase a camp shower. This is a heavy-duty black plastic bag that you fill with water and suspend from a tree or post. The sun heats the water in the bag. While it won't be steamy hot, it is far better than just dumping a bucket of rainwater on your head. The bag has a small hose and nozzle built in so you can direct the water where you wish. I'd suggest putting some sort of container on the ground for you to stand in as you shower so you can collect the runoff water and later reuse it in the garden or something.

Another solution is to set up a ladder and literally have someone dump buckets of water over your head. You could heat the water over a fire to make this a little more comfortable.

For either of these approaches, you might consider draping tarps or even old bed sheets over clotheslines to provide at least a modicum of privacy.

For situations where water is too scarce to allow for actual bathing, you'll have to resort to sponge baths. It might sound absurd, but it is indeed possible to do a decent job of cleaning your body with less than two cups of water. Use the first cup to dampen a washcloth and get a bit of suds going on it with a bar of soap. Wash your body, paying particular attention to underarms, groin, and feet. Then, use a second washcloth and the other cup of water to rinse off. Not the greatest solution, of course, but probably the best under the circumstances.

Stock up on plenty of soap and shampoo to last through the crisis. Remember, it need not be the high-dollar brand-name stuff. You aren't looking for that high-gloss shine; you just want to be clean. One way to perhaps save a few bucks is to ask family and friends to save hotel shampoos and soaps for you when they travel. A friend of a friend of my wife's travels extensively for her job and in just a few months collected a large box of hotel shampoo, body wash, and conditioner.

TOOTH CARE

Toothbrushes are very cheap, and there is no reason you shouldn't be able to put together a large stash of them. Toothpaste isn't all that expensive either if you stick with the store brands. Taking care of your teeth is vitally important, so do everything you can to stock up on the necessary items. Don't forget to floss!

In the event that the supply of toothpaste runs out, you can make a serviceable alternative out of salt and baking soda. Mix together the two ingredients, using one part salt to two parts baking soda. Sprinkle a bit on a toothbrush and brush normally. It won't taste the greatest, but it will work to clean the teeth and gums. This also works better if you first grind the salt with a mortar and pestle or with a rolling pin, then mix with the baking soda.

A good-quality mouthwash might also be desirable. While your supply might not last forever, just a few bottles can last quite a while if you are diligent about rationing them. You can make a serviceable mouthwash by mixing hydrogen peroxide and water in roughly equal quantities. It might not taste minty fresh, but it will certainly do the job. While swishing with alcohol, such as vodka, will kill off bacteria, you're probably better off saving such beverages for trading.

The goal isn't really to have great-smelling breath, but to protect your teeth as best you can. Abscesses and other tooth issues can be not only very painful but also life threatening. You likely won't have ready access

PREPPER'S LONG-TERM SURVIVAL GUIDE

to a dental clinic, either, to help with issues that crop up. If a tooth becomes infected, the only feasible way to handle it might be to remove it from the equation.

FEMININE HYGIENE

Given that close to half of the population has to deal with menstruation, it makes sense to make sure you're prepared in that regard. If you have women in your family or group, make sure you've consulted with them about their specific needs in this arena.

While tampons or pads are typically the go-to products, it might not be practical or feasible to stockpile enough of them for an extreme long-term situation. Focus instead on reusability. The DivaCup is one such option. It is a small, flexible cup made of rubber or silicone that collects the fluids before they leave the body. It is removed and cleaned regularly, of course. This might be something that should be practiced with well in advance, just to make sure there are no negative reactions. Another approach is reusable pads. These can be purchased, or you can sew your own. There are numerous patterns available for free online. Naturally, they'll need to be cleaned after use.

Even if you don't currently have women of childbearing age in your family or group, if you have daughters, keep in mind that they'll grow up, probably sooner than you'd like.

WASTE DISPOSAL

No matter how frugally we live, whether by accident or design, we are going to generate some amount of waste. Currently, most of us put that stuff at the end of the driveway, and it magically disappears every week or so. Other nasty stuff gets sucked down the drains in our homes, hopefully never to be seen again. However, if the garbage collectors aren't visiting anymore, and working flush toilets are nothing but a memory, you're going to have to take care of this waste yourself.

GARBAGE

Perhaps I shouldn't be, but I'm frequently amazed at the amount of garbage the average family generates in just a week. For many households, it is a matter of course to fill up an entire fifty-five-gallon refuse container, often with a bag or two on the side. Part of this stems from living in a disposable society, where few things are made to last, and from the popularity of convenience foods, coming as they do in all manner of boxes and plastic packages.

After a collapse, you'll hopefully be able to burn quite a bit of your refuse. As for the remainder, take a good, long look at it and see if you can come up with a way to repurpose at least some of it. Plastic bowls could be used for plants, for example. Tin cans could be used for DIY alarms by filling them with pebbles and stacking them near doors and other areas so they "sound off" if someone goes by.

The point is to get creative so as to reduce the amount of refuse you truly need to dispose of. Whatever is left will need to be dealt with, of course. Burying it is probably your best option, provided you have the space for doing so. Keep it well away from any natural water sources and bury it at least a few feet deep to keep critters from digging it up.

Another option, if you live in a community, is to set up one specific area to use as a dump. Ideally, this will be on the outskirts of town. Encourage all involved to actively repurpose whatever they can before it makes it to the dump.

HUMAN WASTE

There are a few different things you can do to dispose of human waste that is collected inside the home. The first is to bury it. Dig the

PREPPER'S LONG-TERM SURVIVAL GUIDE

hole at least three feet deep and at least a few hundred feet from any water source. What I suggest doing is digging the hole, then regularly emptying your buckets or whatever you're using for an indoor toilet into the hole. Each time, sprinkle dirt over the waste to help reduce odors. When the waste reaches to within two feet of the top of the hole, fill it in completely. Then, move on to the next location and dig a new hole. This is definitely the option to choose if you're using cat litter or sand in your makeshift toilet.

If you have women who will be adding their used hygiene products to the waste, I'd go a step further and before shoveling in the soil, add a layer of gravel. This will help prevent the smell of blood attracting predators to the area.

The second option is to burn the waste. Ideally, you will first let it dry in the sun for a day or two, then sprinkle on a bit of kerosene or gasoline to make it easy to light. Note that this is not the best solution but will do if you don't have any other feasible options.

You might consider composting human waste, then using it on the gardens. To go this route, you'll want to try and keep the urine separate from the feces. This, of course, will be infinitely easier to do at the time of, ahem, depositing it, rather than after the fact. Use a funnel and some rubber tubing to run the urine into a jug. Urine is high in phosphorous and nitrogen, both nutrients beneficial to plants. Let the urine age for a month or two, then combine it with gray water from your laundry or bathing. Use one part urine to eight parts water to prevent the nitrogen from burning the plant roots. Pour the mixture right into the garden.

The solids (feces, toilet paper) should be collected into a separate pail. When the pail is about full, place a perforated lid on it and let it age for about a year. Then, mix the aged feces in with your other normal compost. Yes, it needs to season for eleven to twelve months. Remember, we're looking to the long term here.

While a number of composting toilets are available for purchase, you may wish to treat this as a DIY project. If that's the case, I highly recommend the Humanure Handbook website, www.HumanureHandbook.com.

CORPSES

If there is a topic even more icky than dealing with human waste, it is corpse disposal. While we hate to lump the bodies of our loved ones into the same category as garbage and human feces, the reality is that something will need to be done with corpses, and odds are pretty good that local funeral homes aren't going to be a feasible option. In the event of a total societal collapse, there will most likely be quite a number of bodies that need attention. Leaving corpses where they lie isn't just a health hazard; it would be a pretty big hit on morale.

The thought of using mass graves isn't something that makes us feel all that great, but it might be the best option, particularly if earth-moving equipment like bulldozers are still operable. Whether it is a mass grave or just an individual one, the same rules generally apply. Dig the grave deep enough to be able to cover it with at least a few feet of soil. Prior to filling in the dirt, if pea gravel is available, put down a layer of that. Doing so will give you some extra insurance that critters won't find the bodies.

Burning is another option, though perhaps even less desirable than mass graves. The problem is that the temperatures required for actual cremation are very high, 1,600°F or so, which is just not feasible in any sort of funeral pyre. But burning will reduce the bodies quite a bit, requiring a smaller grave to be dug.

While we'd want to do what we could to treat bodies with respect, it bears noting that pretty much every religious faith, as well as science, agrees that the body left behind after death is merely the vehicle in which the person had lived. The body isn't really the person anymore.

CHAPTER 6

STAYING WARM AND KEEPING COOL: GIMME SHELTER

Starting to get cold outside. Not too bad—yet—but winter is surely coming. I've been spending at least a few hours every day trying to collect wood we can burn in the fireplace. Of course, most people in the neighborhood are doing the same thing, so the pickings are pretty damn slim.

Speaking of fire, Pacione's house went up the other night. Apparently, Nick was cooking dinner on the grill, and it was pouring rain out so he had the grill up close to the garage, trying to keep things dry under the roof overhang. I guess the roof on that side of the garage was pretty low. There was a big flare-up on the grill, and next thing they knew, smoke and fire were pouring from the garage into the house. The rain managed to contain the fire on the outside, but it didn't do much of anything to stop it inside the house. They all got out OK, thankfully, but they lost pretty much everything. Nick and his two kids are staying with the Taylors for the time being. Many of us were able to donate some clothes and other odds and ends, but I'm not sure how they plan to feed the extra mouths over there.

Clothing in general hasn't been much of an issue, at least for most of us. It is actually sort of nice to not have to worry about "business casual" every day. There are a few folks who seem bound and determined to remain stylish, which, frankly, just comes across as silly. Most of those high-end designer clothes don't seem to be holding up too well to daily life around here. If anything, though, it is shoes that seem to be an issue for most people. Haven't seen any flip-flops for a while, which is NOT a bad thing! I've always hated them. Sneakers are falling apart for a lot of folks. They just weren't made for the daily abuse that comes with working outside. Fortunately, our family all had hiking boots that were already broken in fairly well. Guess we can thank Grandma and Grandpa for that, since it was at their place we did all the hiking earlier this year.

Wish we were still there. If they didn't live 150 miles away, I'd be tempted to make the trip. I'm sure they are doing OK through this crisis. All that acreage, dozens of fruit trees, giant garden…sounds like paradise to me right about now.

Shelter from the elements is one of our most basic needs. Without shelter or clothing, we'd quickly perish from exposure. OK, maybe not within minutes, depending on weather conditions, but without some way to keep rain, wind, or snow off us, we're going to be hurting and miserable.

In the wake of a major disaster, you'll hopefully be able to stay in your own home or, at the least, the home of a family member or trusted friend. Keeping a roof over your head will solve many potential problems. The alternative, bugging out to parts unknown, is rife with likely calamities.

CLOTHING

Proper clothing is your first line of defense against the elements. Most of us have entire closets full of shirts, pants, shoes, and the like. But give some real thought to how practical much of your wardrobe would be for working outdoors.

FASHION VS. COMFORT

While I think we'd all agree that comfort should be more important than style, you might be surprised at how many people who, after being accustomed to dressing to impress, will have a rather difficult time wearing clothing that isn't flattering. Don't get me wrong; I think it's perfectly fine to go out and purchase clothing that is both made to last and made to flatter—provided, of course, your budget allows for doing so.

However, the durability and comfort of your clothing are much more important than if your boots match your belt and if you're showing enough cuff beyond the jacket.

See, here's the thing: You're going to end up wearing what is in your closet, right? I mean, after a collapse, you can't just waltz down to Farm and Fleet and pick up some new boots and a nice jacket. That time will have passed, and you'll be stuck with what you have on hand. If all you have in your dresser are ankle socks that are oh-so-cute but impractical for daily wear, that'll be your own fault.

I'm not saying you need to go out and purchase a complete wardrobe. But, if your closet is filled with nothing but designer suits or dresses, you might want to pick up a few sets of grubbies, lest you find yourself weeding the garden while wearing dress slacks. To the best of my knowledge, Prada doesn't make a whole lot of clothing suitable for working out in the field.

Let's start at the feet and work our way up.

FOOTWEAR

Practical and comfortable footwear is crucial. You should have plenty of thick socks to cushion your feet as well as keep them warm and dry. Wool socks work very well for these purposes. Bear in mind that many socks manufactured today, especially the ones you'll find in the average discount stores, are not going to hold up under harsh use and repeated washing. Instead of bargain hunting, spend the few extra dollars for higher quality.

I suggest you also pick up a pair or two of good work boots, if you don't have them on hand already. Look for thick soles with good tread, preferably with a bit of ankle support. Sneakers might be fine for walking around the house and doing a few chores, but odds are very good you'll be spending a lot more time working outside after a collapse. Plus, you'll likely have to deal with dangerous debris such as broken glass, and the average tennis shoe just isn't going to handle that very well.

If you live in an area that regularly receives significant snowfall, be sure you have snow boots as well. While your normal work boots might be OK in an inch or two of wet, cold, slippery snow, I bet your toes will be pretty numb with any higher accumulations.

After purchasing new boots, be sure to break them in well. Wear them often so they become comfortable. After a disaster, you'll have enough on your plate without having to add blisters and sore ankles to the mix.

BOTTOMS

This brings us to pants and such. For many people, blue jeans are the go-to when it comes to working outside, but you may find yourself regretting that decision when it comes time to wash them by hand, as noted in an earlier chapter. Sure, they are comfortable and generally fairly rugged; they are also very cold, not to mention heavy, when wet and take forever to dry out.

Personally, I prefer cargo pants made of a cotton blend. I like them not for any "tactical" reason, really. I just find them comfortable and the extra pockets are very convenient. The important thing is the pants should be comfortable for working in and should not weigh you down.

WHAT ABOUT CAMOUFLAGE?

I've noticed many preppers and survivalists tend to be heavy on the camo clothing. Let's see, the purpose of camouflage is to...what again? Oh, that's right, help you blend in to the environment. And how exactly does a woodland camo pattern help you blend when you're in the middle of suburbia? Yeah, that's what I thought.

Look, camo clothing can be great to have when you're hunting or on patrol, provided you've matched the camo pattern to your area of operation. That said, you'll likely stick out like a sore thumb if you are the only guy or gal in the area who is wearing it on a regular basis.

If you don't already have a few pairs, pick up some long underwear for use in the cold months. These have advanced quite a bit since we were kids and they are much thinner and more comfortable than back in the day.

You should also have shorts for the warmer seasons. Again, look for durability and comfort rather than how nicely they show off your hips. "Daisy Dukes" and other high-rise shorts aren't the way to go.

Pick up at least a couple belts, even if your pants and shorts fit just fine without them. A belt will be invaluable in helping you carry additional gear. I personally prefer leather belts, but fabric ones are fine as well.

TOPS

If there is one item of clothing we all likely have in abundance, it is shirts and sweaters, right? OK, some of the women out there might have more shoes than shirts, but when you add the male members of the population, that average skews toward tops. As I've been saying all along, durability and comfort take precedence over brand name and style. You're going to want a good mix of short-sleeve T-shirts, long-sleeve T-shirts, button-down shirts like flannels, and thicker sweaters or sweatshirts.

UNDERWEAR

Some people might consider underwear something of a luxury. I mean, how far down the list of priorities should this particular item fall? Probably somewhere between food and a way to power your MP3 player, I reckon. That said, underwear serves to help wick moisture away from an already pretty warm area of the body, which can help with reducing skin irritation. For many of us, wearing underclothes is just more comfortable, too. For those who have bits that can bounce or dangle, proper undies can make running and other activity much easier.

Now, there's probably little need to go out and buy numerous packages of new underwear as a stockpile for the future. What I would suggest, though, is if you regularly find yourself running out of clean ones by the end of the week, you might want to augment your supply just a bit. Shoot for having enough to last you at least two weeks. Doing so will help cut down on the frequency of having to do laundry after a disaster.

Don't forget long underwear for colder weather—modern versions are lighter and more comfortable than the older counterparts.

THE PREPPER'S CLOSET

Spring/Summer
- loose-fitting, light-colored shirts
- durable shorts
- wide-brimmed hat

Fall/Winter
- flannel shirts
- long-sleeve T-shirts (for layering)
- thick socks
- knit hat
- gloves/mittens
- warm boots
- balaclava/face mask
- medium-weight jacket
- heavy coat

OUTERWEAR

You've likely noticed by now that a running theme with most of the clothing categories has been to prepare yourself for spending a lot more time outdoors than you might be currently. In a long-term scenario, you can expect to be doing things like gardening, hauling water, chopping and stacking firewood, and other such chores. Therefore, you'll be out in the elements a lot more frequently and for long periods of time.

Outerwear is your "suit of armor," so to speak, protecting you from the wind, rain, and snow.

If you typically just make a mad dash from the front door to your car, pulling out of a driveway you paid to have plowed, you might not already have adequate outerwear. I'm always amazed at the number of people who live near me, in an area that regularly hits -20°F with the wind chill in the winter, who do not even own a heavy coat. If this is you, please pay close attention to this section.

Keeping your head covered is one of the best ways to prevent heat loss. Think of your head as a chimney, with your body heat rising out of it like smoke from a crackling fire. A wool knit cap will keep that heat in, even when wet. If you live in an area that experiences severe cold, you might want to add a face mask or balaclava to the mix.

Mittens are warmer than gloves but are less practical for doing chores. Either way, make sure you keep your hands covered and warm. Remember that scene in the movie *A Christmas Story* where the little boy gets his tongue stuck to the flagpole? That can happen just as easily to hands if they are slightly damp from sweat.

LAYERING

You've probably heard many times the sage advice to dress in layers when it is cold outside. This is especially important when you are exerting yourself—chopping or stacking firewood or conducting security patrols, for example. As you work, your body heats up. What you want to avoid is soaking your inner clothing with sweat. What will happen is that once you're done working, or if you take a break, in cold weather that sweat may turn to ice, or at the least get very, very cold.

By having layers, you can remove clothing as you warm up, then bundle up when you cool down. Layers also serve to keep you warmer in general. They trap air between your shirts and such, which insulates you from the cold.

Those cheap rain ponchos you can buy at the dollar store are only slightly better than a garbage bag with a hole for your head to go through. You should spend a bit more cash to get something durable and comfortable. A hood is a necessity with rain gear, too.

For heavy winter outerwear, I suggest you pick up a good parka. You'll want something that has some freedom of movement and isn't so bulky you feel like the Pillsbury dough boy. Bonus points for one that has a removable liner, allowing you to adjust the degree of warmth to suit the weather. While you should expect to spend in the three digits for quality outerwear, it should also last quite a while. Look at it this way: If you spend $150 on a good parka, and it lasts you five years, you've invested $30 a year. That's not a bad deal.

HOME IS WHERE THE SHELTER IS

Moving on to structures, your home will most likely be your primary shelter in a long-term crisis. After all, it has a roof, walls, and perhaps even insulation to boot. However, as people turn to more primitive means of keeping warm, since odds are pretty good those space heaters and furnaces aren't going to be working, there is an increased risk of house fires. Add to that risk the fact that fire departments will be a thing of the past and you have the makings for yet one more disaster on top of the original one.

Smoke detectors and alarms are critical. Make sure you have one in or near the kitchen and near bedrooms. I also suggest having one in the furnace room. Test them at least twice a year and keep a good supply of batteries on hand for replacements. Since few of your other gadgets will use the typical nine-volt batteries used in the detectors, it shouldn't be too difficult to keep the extras from wandering off.

Make sure you also have one or more fire extinguishers in the kitchen. Put them somewhere easily accessible in an emergency. A box of baking soda will work well at putting out grease fires. Never dump water on a grease fire as it will just cause it to spatter and spread.

This should be common sense, but never use any open-flame source of heating inside the home, unless it is inside a fireplace or woodstove. Proper ventilation is key to preventing carbon monoxide poisoning. If you have a fireplace or woodstove, be sure to clean the chimney every season. Chimney sweeping is not a difficult chore, provided you have the right equipment and can get on your roof safely. It's something you should learn how to do now so you know what you're doing later.

Another consideration is adding at least a few tarps to your preps. These will be handy in the event of damage to the roof or windows of

BASIC CHIMNEY SWEEPING

To perform this necessary chore, you'll need to invest in a chimney brush and rods for it. Before heading to the store, take a close look at the chimney, preferably from the top down. You'll need to know if it is square or round on the inside as well as the dimensions of the opening (hint: bring a tape measure up there with you). You'll also need to know the height of the chimney to determine how many rods you'll need.

For safety, you should wear safety glasses and perhaps a face mask. Work gloves are also recommended.

To clean the chimney, first close off the front of the fireplace or woodstove to keep the dust and soot from going everywhere. Then, go up on the roof and insert the brush, scrubbing up and down. Attach more rods as you work your way to the bottom of the chimney. Use a flashlight to make sure you loosen as much of the soot and creosote on the sides of the chimney as you can.

You can also start cleaning from the bottom and work your way to the top. But this is infinitely dirtier, and you will, without a doubt, get soot on anything near the fireplace you haven't covered with a drop cloth.

Once you have all that debris removed from the chimney, sweep it out of the fireplace.

your home. Use paracord to tie them off, rather than bungee cords. If you have a tarp with a grommet torn out, you can improvise by placing a small rock on the edge or corner of the tarp, folding the tarp over or around the rock, then tying the cord around the bulge.

KEEPING WARM WITHOUT FIRE

Of course, many people have homes without fireplaces or woodstoves, which is certainly not ideal. If you fall into this category, there are a few things you can do to still keep warm.

First, do what you can to keep the family contained to one or two rooms. If you have a two-story home, close off the upper level completely. By congregating together, the combined body heat will do wonders at chasing off chills.

Have plenty of blankets on hand, of course. By huddling under a couple blankets, groups of two or three should be fine.

An old trick is to heat bricks, wrap them in towels, and place them under the blankets. Just be sure you use fire-safe bricks to avoid having them crack and crumble. Large stones could work as well, provided you don't gather them from a riverbank or lakeshore, lest they contain water that will heat to steam and possibly cause the rocks to explode. Hot pads or oven gloves should be used for handling the bare bricks prior to wrapping them up. You could also use hot-water bottles in a similar manner.

KEEPING COOL OFF THE GRID

So far, we've been concentrating our discussion on ways to keep warm and dry after a collapse. But what if the problem isn't cold but extreme heat? After all, getting overheated can be just as serious as being too cold.

Our bodies are designed to work best within a certain ambient temperature range. For most people, this range is about 65°F to 80°F. If it's much cooler than that, then you're looking for a jacket; much hotter, then you're not looking to move around a whole lot. So, how can you beat the heat in the summer months when the air conditioner isn't doing anything but taking up window space?

First, try to complete necessary chores in the early morning or late evening, when the temperature is cooler. Whenever possible, avoid strenuous activity during the hottest hours of the day. Take frequent breaks and make sure you're drinking plenty of water to stay hydrated.

If you have one available, rig up a patio umbrella near where you'll be working so you have some shade. Wearing a wide-brimmed hat will help keep the sun off your face and neck.

Light-colored clothing will keep you much cooler than dark shirts and pants and cotton is cooler than heavier fabrics. A thin cotton scarf or bandana draped on the back of your neck and wetted down will also help keep you cooler. Evaporation is a cooling process; that's why we sweat. By lightly misting your skin from time to time, you can use evaporation to cool down.

Moving into the home, it is important to do what you can to keep the interior cool during the day. Our bodies don't rest very well when they get overly warm. Further, our bodies require adequate amounts of good sleep to keep healthy. If we go too long without decent sleep, whether from the heat or some other reason, our bodies aren't given the chance to recover from the day's work.

Keep drapes and curtains closed during the day to keep out the sun. Open the windows in the evening to let in cooler air. This works best if you have multiple windows across the room from one another so as to allow for cross-ventilation. Consider adding insulation to your attic and walls if they're not already insulated. While this might sound counterintuitive, since we usually think of insulation as keeping things warm, what this does is prevent any cool air in the home from leaking out. Plus, this will obviously also help in the winter with keeping you warmer.

You might also consider planting a few trees on the east and west sides of the home. As they grow, they will provide shade. This will mean, of course, that you'll need to be vigilant about keeping the trees healthy. A large, dead tree falling on the home during a grid-down scenario won't be much fun.

While this suggestion might be a no-brainer, given the probable lack of working ovens and microwaves, do as much cooking outside as possible. By keeping heat sources outside the home, you'll not be heating the room as well as the food.

Heat rises, so if you live in a two-story home, close off the upper level if you can. What you might want to do, though, is open the windows upstairs during the day to allow the heat up there to escape.

¤ ¤ ¤ ¤

While most of us likely have a closet full of clothing and a roof over our heads, we should still give thought to shelter issues when planning for long-term survival. We need to be prepared to take care of that roof, make necessary repairs, and have the proper safety equipment in place.

Working outdoors is something many may not be used to. As a result, they might not already have the necessary attire. Investing as little as forty dollars at a thrift store can get you fixed up quite well in that regard.

CHAPTER 7

SECURITY: YOU CAN NEVER HAVE ENOUGH DEFENSE

We spend a great deal of our days and nights feeling at least some degree of fear and anxiety. It seems like a lifetime ago, even though it has only been a few months, that a knock on the door likely meant someone trying to sell cheap siding after a hailstorm or perhaps an earnest youth wanting to take a moment to share with us the word of his Savior. Today, not even Jehovah's Witnesses are going door to door, and visitors with the most innocent of intents are seen first as potential aggressors, or "brigands," as Bill down the road insists on calling them. He probably has less to fear than most of us, given that pack of malamutes he has at his place. I shudder to think what he's been having to feed them.

There have been several violent encounters, particularly in the early days. Once the punks and ne'er-do-wells realized they needn't fear the police showing up to spoil their fun, the kid gloves came off. There were home invasions, assaults, and much worse. The easy targets were first—the elderly living alone and the single mothers. The rest of us were still trying to get our own bearings and didn't act quickly enough. If we'd been better prepared, maybe we could have saved a few more lives. I think a lot about Susie, who lived a few blocks from us. Her two young kids are going to need a lifetime of therapy, assuming a therapist still exists somewhere. Susie wouldn't have hurt a fly. She was just a mom trying to get by and provide for her kids. At least she isn't in pain anymore... Once we finally got our feet back underneath us, though, we took action. Given that I have no way to know who may read this or when, I'll only say the initial attackers were...handled. Or at least those we knew where to find. I'm sure several got away, and most of us fear what will happen if they return in larger numbers.

But it isn't just the "normal" criminals we fear. More and more, even longtime neighbors are becoming desperate. Food is scarce, as is everything else. Today, I have enough to keep my family fed. But what if I didn't? How long could I sit here and watch my loved ones starve before I felt I had to do something, anything, to put food in their stomachs? How far would I go? It terrifies me to think I might find out...

Security and defense are, or should be, among your chief concerns for extended survival scenarios. Having enough food and water to last years isn't going to do you a lick of good if someone can easily take them from you. Also worth noting is the fact that most, if not all, residential security systems in common use today are designed to notify the authorities in the event of a home invasion or other situation. The breaking of a window trips an alarm that results in a police officer being dispatched to the residence. That idea generally works well when times are normal.

When times are not normal, though, calling 911 will be nothing more than a memory. The thought of a squad car racing down the road, lights blazing and siren blaring, will be fantasy at best. If you hear a window break at 2:00 a.m., it is up to you, and only you, to find out what is going on and handle it appropriately.

Your security planning should involve several elements, including defensive weapons, structure hardening, alarm devices, and, above all, situational awareness. But before we get into all that, first things first.

OPSEC AND BEING THE GRAY MAN

OPSEC stands for operations security. This used to be strictly a military term referring to the protection of information that could be used to harm the troops. In the last couple of decades, the term was co-opted by the prepper and survivalist folks, many of whom are veterans. In essence, it boils down to keeping your mouth shut. The fewer the people who know anything about your preps, the fewer the number of people who may show up with their hands out later. An obvious violation of OPSEC would be bragging about your pallets of canned goods when you're down at the bowling alley. A perhaps less obvious violation would be receiving several packages via UPS every single week, all prominently labeled with the name of some emergency gear outfitter. Believe me when I say that neighbors notice things like this and many tend to have long memories. A much better solution would be to stagger your shipments so they come less frequently, or have them shipped to an alternate location such as a post office box or your workplace, or only do business with companies who ship in unmarked boxes.

The preps you store within the home, your canned goods and bottled water, should not be left out in plain sight. The guy who comes in to fix your furnace should not get a guided tour of your pantry storage on his way to the basement. Keep your preps under wraps as best you can. Choose an area of your basement, for example, that gets little use now. Build shelving for the supplies, then use curtains over the front and sides of the shelves to keep things out of sight. I know, it sounds sort of stupid, but trust me, it works. If someone were to ever question it, just tell them you were sick of looking at all the cardboard boxes and wanted to brighten up the area with some color.

OPSEC also extends to the period of time we're focusing on—the aftermath of a major collapse. If three months have gone by since the grid went down, you don't want to be the lone person in the neighborhood who has actually gained weight while everyone else is starving. I'm not suggesting you starve yourself just to fit in, but use a bit of common sense. Let your clothing sag a bit on your frame so it is less obvious that you've missed far fewer meals than your neighbors. A generally disheveled appearance, with unkempt hair and unshaven face, can also go a long way toward helping you fit into the crowd.

That's what we call being the "Gray Man." Blending into the neighborhood, not standing out in a crowd, is the objective. Granted, your neighbors know who you are and will probably notice you when you're out and about. However, you don't want to look out of place when compared to them. This actually can be a difficult concept for some people to grasp. Many folks spend a large portion of their lives wanting to stand out, wanting to be the "main attraction" in the circus that is their neighborhood. Keeping up with the Joneses and all that. Having a nicer car, bigger pool, and more expensive clothing might be fun now so you can one-up those snots across the street. But when your neighbors are having to scrounge for their next meal, the last thing you want is for them to believe you have something they do not.

DEFENSIVE WEAPONS

We humans have used weapons of one sort or another since the first cave dweller bonked another over the head with a stick. Weapons are used to increase our reach, our strength, and our overall capacity to defend ourselves. Weapons are tools, nothing more and nothing less. They are a means to achieving a goal, that being to defend yourself and your loved ones. Weapons are not inherently evil, and they lack the capacities of thought and intent. A firearm, for example, is not going to differentiate between an intruder and your teenage son sneaking in after curfew. It is up to the user to exercise the necessary judgment to ensure the weapon is used appropriately.

I go through all that in hopes of allaying the very natural fears of those people who are new to firearms and other weapons. If the thought of visiting violence upon another person, no matter how deserved it may be, disturbs you, then congratulations! That means you're a human being. Most of us do not relish the thought of deliberately injuring someone else.

The unfortunate fact, though, is there are people out there (and I use the term "people" rather loosely) who will not think twice about causing injury or death to others for the sole purpose of taking what their victims have, whether it be food, valuables, or even their bodies. That's the case now, in relatively safe times, and even more so if there is little to no threat of being arrested.

While a baseball bat can make for a very expedient weapon, it isn't going to do much good against a handgun or rifle. As the old saying goes, "Don't bring a knife to a gunfight." If you do not already own one or more firearms, your first goal should be to legally acquire one.

That, of course, raises the question of what firearms are best suited for defense. There are as many answers are there are gun owners. Everyone has their own favorites and can make very compelling arguments why their choice is better than the rest. There are basically four different types of firearms that are well suited for defense: handguns, shotguns, long rifles, and carbines.

HANDGUNS

Selecting handguns, perhaps more than other types of firearms, really comes down to personal preference. If the gun isn't comfortable in your hands to hold or shoot, you won't practice with it like you should, and you'll never become proficient with it as a result. This means you may need to test out several before finding one that "fits."

On top of the comfort issue is the price. Investing in a gun (or in several) is not a cheap endeavor. A low-end handgun will run you around three bills, so it is wise to do your homework and test out several different ones before making a selection.

Handguns come in two different flavors: semi-automatic and revolver. As with anything else, each has pros and cons. The semi-autos will generally carry more ammunition in the magazine than you'll have in a revolver, giving you more shots before reloading. But they can be a bit more complicated overall. A revolver, on the other hand, while giving you fewer rounds, might be easier to use for someone new to firearms.

TO SHOOT OR NOT TO SHOOT

Neither I nor anyone else can give you definite, concrete guidelines to follow in deciding if and when to actually pull the trigger. But I can give you the following advice.

First, be damn sure of your target. Shooting in low-light conditions, while under stress, can cause you to see funny things. You need to be 100 percent confident you know whom or what you are shooting at, as well as what lies behind the target. The last thing you want is for an errant round to strike a family member crouching behind the aggressor. Remember, a bullet cannot be called back once it leaves the barrel. Once the trigger is pulled, it is too late for a do-over.

Second, even if there is effectively no law and order at the moment, that doesn't mean it won't ever be reestablished. When that happens, authorities may decide to investigate what happened during the "bad times." Keep in mind that it's rather difficult for a corpse to corroborate your version of events.

Third, if, at the conclusion of the confrontation, you and your loved ones are safe, odds are pretty good you did the right thing.

As for handgun calibers, I suggest you stick to common ones such as .357, 9mm, .40, or .45. The more obscure the caliber, the harder it will be to find ammunition, now or later.

The advantages of using handguns for defense include their ease of carry as well as ease of use. It is vastly easier to go about your daily routine with a handgun on your hip than with a shotgun strapped to your back. You can also carry a substantial amount of extra ammunition (whether in magazines for semi-autos or speedloaders for revolvers) without feeling like a pack mule.

However, handguns have limited range and, for some at least, require a considerable amount of practice to become truly accurate with them at any distance. But, then again, if an intruder were to gain access to your home, what would be the longest distance from which you'd have to hit your target? I doubt most homes have hallways longer than, say, thirty feet.

SHOTGUNS

Some might say shotguns are tailor-made for home defense. They are brutally effective at close range and also somewhat forgiving to the shooter's accuracy or lack thereof, due to how shot spreads upon leaving the barrel.

With a little shopping around, you can secure a decent, used 12-gauge shotgun for under a few hundred dollars. The ammunition is commonly sold at most sporting goods stores. While a shotgun isn't the lightest weapon available, most people should be able to handle one comfortably with a little practice. If you are slight of frame, you might consider downgrading to a 20-gauge, as it will have a bit less recoil.

RIFLES

Rifles are generally for distance shooting. Where a 12-gauge shotgun shooting 00 buckshot will have an effective range of about thirty-five to forty yards, a deer rifle like a 30.06 will be quite lethal to large game (including two-legged targets) at well over two hundred yards. That said, go outside your home and visualize two football fields end to end, in each direction. Unless you live far out into the boonies, I doubt you'll be able to see many targets quite that far away. However, these high-powered rifles are great for harvesting large game should the opportunity present itself. Further, equipped with a scope and some experience, someone stationed on the roof of your home or another high point should be able to keep varmints of all shapes and sizes from getting too close.

There is also something to be said for the lowly .22 rifle. This is, to my way of thinking, perhaps the most versatile of the survival firearms.

If you shop around and pay attention to advertisements, you can pick up a great Ruger 10/22 for just over a couple hundred dollars. The ammunition, despite a small increase in price in recent years, is still fairly cheap. The .22 is a great hunting rifle, handling just about anything up to and including deer (if you are particularly skilled). The maximum effective range of the .22LR round is about 100 to 120 yards.

Some people feel the .22 is too low powered to serve adequately for defensive purposes. To them I say, if you feel that confident, how about you take a .22LR round in the knee at about fifty yards? I'm willing to bet you'll change your mind. The ideal, of course, would be a higher caliber round. But, if all you have to spend on firearms is a few hundred dollars, start with a Ruger 10/22 and a stash of ammunition with which to practice. As the budget allows, increase the armory.

CARBINES

Strictly speaking, carbines fall into the rifle category but given their popularity among preppers, I felt they deserved their own section. A carbine, by traditional definition, is nothing more than a short rifle. Umpteen years ago, they were developed for ease of use while on horseback. Today, they have sort of acquired a life of their own. Many, though certainly not all, of the dreaded "black guns" that have been demonized in the media fall into the carbine category. They are often militaristic in appearance, with magazines holding up to a couple dozen rounds or so.

The upside to carbines is the increased capacity as well as the intimidation factor. The downside is the cost. Carbines can easily run into the several-hundred-dollar range, and the ammunition isn't cheap either. However, the AR-15, firing 5.56mm rounds, will certainly do well toward causing a pants-filling moment for any intruder. Just remember what I said before about overpenetration.

The SKS carbine is another great option. Firing the 7.62×39mm round, it packs a lot of power into a manageable size. Most of the AK variants are known for their durability and reliability, both of which are excellent traits for the prepper.

HOW MUCH IS TOO MUCH?

As many, many people have discovered, buying firearms and ammunition for them can be somewhat addicting. You may start with just wanting a small handgun for personal defense, but before you know it, you're saving up for that really cool-looking AR hanging in the store's case. It is frighteningly easy to end up with tunnel vision and focus all your efforts on increasing the armory, while neglecting the other important areas of prepping.

With that in mind, my suggestion is to set a specific goal with regards to armaments. Once that goal is reached, concentrate your efforts on the other aspects of preparedness, while always keeping an eye out for deals that might fall into your lap.

The ideal minimum would be for each mature member of your family or group to have a handgun and a rifle, carbine, or shotgun. Notice I did not specify "adult" but rather "mature." I've met teenagers who have much more common sense than some grown-ups, so base your decisions on the individual's maturity level and intelligence, not birth date. As for ammunition, well, without ammo, your firearms will be nothing more than weird-looking clubs, so err on the side of excess in that regard. Better to have too many rounds than be even one short. For handguns, let's say 1,000 rounds at a minimum. Rifles and carbines, 5,000 rounds. Shotguns, maybe 2,500 shells. The reason this is skewed toward rifles is they will be used for hunting as well as protection. While it is possible to hunt with a handgun, I don't recommend it unless you are fairly adept.

NON-FIREARM WEAPONRY

Remember what I said earlier about bringing a knife to a gunfight? The same holds true for bringing baseball bats, swords, throwing stars, and axes. You are far better off concentrating your efforts on legally acquiring firearms than you are stocking up on medieval or martial arts weapons, no matter how much of a "cool factor" they might have.

However, if there is one non-firearm weapon I would suggest, it would be a good-quality knife. A knife is probably the most useful tool you can carry with you, and it just happens to make for a decent weapon. While anything sharp and pointy is going to be better than empty hands, a knife really isn't something to skimp on. Expect to part with more than a few shekels to purchase a decent knife that will be suitable for defense.

The blade should be around five to six inches in length. This will give you good penetration while not being cumbersome. You want a knife that has a full *tang*. This means the blade actually runs all the way through the handle of the knife as a solid piece of metal. A full-tang knife is infinitely stronger than one that just has the blade screwed into the handle. Blade thickness is also important. The thinner the spine of the blade, the weaker the knife will be. The blade itself should be made of high-carbon steel. This gives you the hardness you want in order to retain the sharp edge, while still allowing you to touch up that edge as needed.

As for the handle material, look for something that will help you retain your grip should the knife become wet. This is important whether the wetness is from blood or from rain. The sheath should be comfortable to wear for extended periods of time. Personally, I prefer leather sheaths, but I'm admittedly a bit old-fashioned in that regard. Kydex sheaths are a great alternative to leather. Nylon sheaths are OK, but, in my experience, most aren't made to last or hold up under abuse.

While any sharp knife can be a potential weapon, if you're going to invest in a cutting tool for defense, it should be designed for that purpose. Here's a short list of makers I'd recommend:

- Spartan Blades (SpartanBladesUSA.com)
- RMJ Tactical (RMJTactical.com)
- Toor Knives (ToorKnives.com)
- TOPS Knives (TOPSKnives.com)
- Vehement Knives (VehementKnives.com)

STRUCTURE HARDENING

As you work on assembling your armaments, you should also look at your home itself, with an eye toward increasing defensibility. The idea here is not necessarily to turn your home into a fortified bunker, as few people would wish to live in such an environment. However, short of that, there are several things you can do now that will dramatically increase your survivability in a postcollapse world.

First, recognize the weak points in your home. These are the doors and windows. Your first step is to do what you can to strengthen those entry points. Start by replacing the hinge screws in your exterior doors. Most doors are installed with relatively short screws that do nothing other than support the door in the frame. Take those out, one at a time, and replace them with screws that are long enough to penetrate through the frame and go into the studs, figure about three inches or so.

If the exterior doors don't have dead bolts, purchase and install one for each door. Be sure the bolt extends into the door frame by at least an inch or more. Use this dead bolt each and every time you lock the door. Getting into the habit now will save you from having to remember when it truly counts.

You could also spend a couple bucks on a few 2×4 or 2×6 boards and, when needed, screw those down across those doors that open inward.

This isn't something you'd want to do over and over again, of course, but this is a cheap and easy way to augment the security of exterior doors if you find yourself needing to barricade yourself inside.

Windows are problematic because, well, they're made of glass. What you might want to do is take some measurements and then head to your local lumberyard and purchase half- or three-quarter-inch plywood sheets to cover the inside of each window. You wouldn't want to do it now, of course, but having them precut and ready to go will save you time later. Using those same size screws you used on the door hinges, you'll affix the plywood over the inside of each window. Be sure the screws dig into studs and not just wallboard. Store these pieces in the garage or attic until you need to use them.

Sandbags are another tool you can use. They need not be made of canvas, nor filled with sand. The idea behind sandbags is to provide mass that will absorb a bullet's impact. A stack or two of bags of soil purchased at your local garden center will do nicely in a pinch. These bags could be positioned in various parts of the house, say in front of upper-level windows, to provide a makeshift firing position.

PERIMETER DEFENSE

The term "perimeter" refers to the area extending outward from the walls of your home and includes the area that you can reasonably expect to defend. This will vary based on several factors, such as the size of your yard and the firearms available to you. For example, if all you have is a couple handguns, you aren't defending a perimeter that extends much beyond the average suburban front yard. You just won't have the range with those weapons to reach that far. On the other hand, if you have a high-caliber deer rifle and the ability to hit a target accurately at distance, you could look at extending that perimeter beyond your front sidewalk.

The purpose of implementing perimeter defense is to hopefully prevent small problems from developing into larger ones. Think of defense in terms of layers, like an onion. The outer layer is your perimeter. Second layer is your structure. Third and innermost layer is yourself.

Perimeter defense consists of two primary elements: early-warning systems and devices to discourage further efforts on the part of the intruders.

EARLY-WARNING SYSTEMS

Anything you can do to decrease the amount of time it takes to detect an intruder will give you more time to react efficiently. Therefore, you want to do what you can to implement some sort of alarms or other warning devices. This could be as simple as rigging up strings of bells or tin cans filled with pebbles in strategic locations. One idea worth noting is to place brush or large debris along primary routes through your yard, such as along the back side of the garage or shed. Then, run a string or some fishing line from the brush to your string of bells. The intruder may move the brush aside to make room for himself, which will then cause the bells to chime.

A visit to your local Radio Shack or other electronics retailer can provide you with battery-operated alarms, such as motion sensors. Assuming you have a way to keep them powered, these can work very well. If you go this route, I suggest you play around with them a bit to find the best locations not only for detection but also for ease of hearing the alarm when it goes off.

TRAPS AND FUNNELING

Because I'm nothing if not a fourteen-year-old boy at heart, and the term "booby trap" still makes me giggle, let's just refer to them as traps. While the thought of turning your backyard into one big, live-action version of the game Mousetrap might sound like fun, that would be an awful lot of work and, let's face it, would make a trip to the garden arduous at best. Instead, focus your efforts on using traps to funnel your potential intruders to areas you can better defend.

What do I mean by funneling? This refers to forcing intruders to stay out of hidden areas and move into locations where they are better targets for you. Human beings are largely creatures of habit. We will usually take the easiest route possible to get from Point A to Point B. If the direct line between those points is rife with debris or other potentially nasty stuff, we'll deviate from it rather than continue on course. Use this tendency to your advantage and place hidden, or maybe even not-so-hidden traps to force them to move to more visible areas.

Let's say you have a space behind a garden shed you want to keep people from hiding behind. Dig a shallow ditch, just a few inches deep, along the back of the shed. Cut sections of plywood to fit the length and width of the ditch. Drive several long nails or screws into the plywood and then place the board into the ditch with the screws facing up. Toss in some doggie doo for good measure, then cover the whole thing with grass or leaves.

SITUATIONAL AWARENESS

An important element, perhaps the most important, of any security plan is situational awareness. This is, essentially, taking the blinders off and seeing the great, big world around you. If you walk or drive down the street today, you'll notice a plethora of pedestrians with their faces buried in cell phones. Quite literally, you could smack them in the shoulder, and they'd likely not notice. They are entirely too entranced in checking email or watching the latest Disney starlet who has gone on to flaunt her stuff on a stripper pole. This is precisely the opposite of situational awareness.

In the aftermath of a major event, you want to be hyperaware of anyone coming within a fair distance of your home. This includes both strangers as well as your neighbors. While one would hope those you've known and trusted for years aren't going to show up with ill intent, you need to modify your thinking a bit and instead assume the worst until proven otherwise.

Strangers should always be seen as security risks. I'm not suggesting you shoot first and forget questions entirely, but anyone not known to you and your family should not be allowed to approach the home unchallenged. If they are looking for a handout, well, I won't act as your conscience, but suffice to say that any food you give out lessens your ability to provide for your family.

Also, be aware of diversions. A group may send a young child toward a home under the pretense of asking for help, while the remaining members work their way to the sides and back in hopes of facilitating a surprise attack. Any time someone is observed in the immediate area of the home, residents should be on high alert.

Ideally, you should have enough people within your home that at least one person can act as something of a lookout at all times. Stagger sleep times if need be to ensure someone is always awake and watching for danger. You aren't just concentrating on watching for intruders either, but any and all dangers such as fires.

If you don't have the luxury of several people to rotate in shifts, consider giving a home to a canine companion. A well-trained mutt can do the job of a couple people when it comes to alerting you to danger. Plus, they are awfully warm during cold winter nights.

CONSEQUENCES

When we talk about prepping, we typically focus on what to do before, during, and immediately after a disaster hits. After all, the word "prepping" comes from the word "prepare," right? We prepare for emergencies, for disasters, for life's little (and not-so-little) curve balls.

CHARITY SURVIVAL KITS

Undoubtedly, some folks out there will have a hard time turning away people who obviously are in really bad shape. If you fall into that camp, you might consider putting together what we could call charity survival kits. Of course, this is predicated upon you having sufficient stockpiles of food and gear that you can afford to give a little away.

Suggestions on what to include in such a kit:

- a couple cans of food with a small folding can opener
- two or three bottles of water
- a handful of strike-anywhere matches in a waterproof container
- one or two emergency blankets
- directions to the nearest emergency shelter, if one has been set up in the area
- a pair of clean socks

These sorts of kits could be stashed at a local church or abandoned building. If you're approached by someone needing help, you can mention that someone in town has been putting charity kits at that location, so they could check there.

What is often not discussed is the fact that disasters don't go on forever. At some point, order is restored. And when that happens, there may be some pushback, perhaps even consequences, for actions taken during the crisis.

That neighbor you thumbed your nose at when they asked for help? They managed to make it through and are still living next door. That'll be a fun conversation when you both happen to be taking out the trash bins at the same time.

That guy you shot in the backyard who had committed the grievous crime of daring to set foot on your property? Criminal charges have now been filed against you, and his family is suing you to boot.

That house you raided for supplies when the owners seemed to be absent? They've since returned and would really like to speak with you about the things you took, particularly the firearms, as well as the damage caused to the back door.

All of this is to say that far too many preppers and survivalists appear eager to be trigger-pullers the moment society starts to look even slightly off-kilter. While desperate times might call for desperate measures, bear in mind that at some point you may be called upon to answer for those measures taken. Maybe don't be so eager to engage in behavior that could prove problematic down the road. Plan ahead so your actions are reasonable and appropriate, rather than forced by a lack of other options.

CHAPTER 8

TOOLS: HE WHO SURVIVES WITH THE MOST TOYS WINS

One of my father's more popular sayings was "Use the right tool for the right job." His garage always looked like a Sears showroom, with pegboard completely covering three walls and jam-packed with every tool imaginable. Many a time over the last several months I've longed to have access to that tool collection again.

For the most part, we've been able to make do with what we have. A few people in the neighborhood have pretty large assortments of tools, and, thankfully, they've been pretty decent about letting others borrow them for limited times. The rest of us, though, don't have much to use. A few screwdrivers, maybe an adjustable wrench, at best a small toolbox filled with odds and ends accumulated over a decade or more of buying something cheap to do a particular job around the house.

Things would be so much easier if we still had power, of course. Cordless drills and drivers are looked upon wistfully as we try to drive screws by hand. Nails have become much more popular than screws for that very reason. Seems like everyone has a hammer at least.

The gardens we've been expanding are also all being dug and tilled by hand. Back-breaking work, but many of us are finding calluses replacing blisters by now. Personally, I am actually enjoying working with my hands and seeing the results of my efforts. Watching the garden take shape, knowing it is my blood and sweat forming it, really is good for my soul. It helps offset everything else that has gone wrong.

Humans aren't the only animals on the planet who use tools, but, as far as I know, we're the only ones who've gone so far as to make tools for others to buy. The garage described above is very similar to the one I grew up with. My dad has owned so many tools, I'm convinced he bought a fair number of them without even truly knowing their purpose.

But, damn, if they didn't look good hanging on the pegboard. And, if that purpose ever arose, he had the perfect tool for the job.

Now, tools may not be as important as, say, food or water, in your overall prep planning. But make no mistake, in a long-term grid-down scenario, you'll need all the assistance you can get. Having the foresight to amass a decent collection of tools will do nothing but help.

What follows is a discussion of the tools that might become necessary after a collapse. I'm not suggesting you drop everything, head to Home Depot, and spend a gazillion dollars buying all this stuff. However, I do recommend going through your own tool collection, such as it may be, and making a list of the ones you don't already own. Keep that list handy as you hit rummage sales, flea markets, and leaf through sale ads. Pick up the tools here and there as you can afford to do so.

GENERAL REPAIRS

During the time that you are truly on your own, calling a plumber or carpenter to take care of basic household repairs isn't going to be an

SPEND THE MONEY FOR QUALITY

It is very possible, even likely, that your life or welfare will depend upon the tools you purchase. Therefore, spend the money to get decent ones. Avoid any tools that are sold in dollar stores; most of them aren't even worth the buck. Personally, I look for brand names like Craftsman and Stanley. Even the house brands at big-box home improvement stores, like Kobalt tools at Lowe's, are fairly good. If you shop around, watching the sale ads as well as haunting rummage sales, you can find good stuff at decent prices.

With rummage sales, in particular, you can come across some great bargains. I'd gladly clean a little rust off a forty-year-old set of Craftsman wrenches if I can buy the whole set for ten bucks.

option. You're going to need to handle things yourself, and, to do so, you'll need some basic tools.

Hammers come in a surprising number of variations. Just your basic claw hammer will have different models, styles, and weights. While you're in the store, play around with them a little bit. Look for one that isn't too heavy for you to control easily. The handle should fit snugly into the head, with absolutely no wiggle room. Personally, I prefer a hickory handle, but as long as it is comfortable in your hands, you should be fine. You'll want at least two hammers, so you'll have a backup as well as the ability to have two people working on a job together.

You're also going to want multiple screwdrivers, both slotted and Phillips, and different sizes for different screws. There is little that is more frustrating in life than trying to turn a screw with a screwdriver that is just a hair too big or too small.

While you could maybe get by with an adjustable wrench or two, having a set of metric and standard (SAE) open/box-end wrenches (also known as combination wrenches) will make your life much easier. Get a set of each, then toss in a couple adjustable wrenches for good measure.

Pliers likewise come in a dazzling array of shapes and sizes. I've managed to get by with having two pairs of ten-inch slip-joint pliers and a couple smaller ones. Needle-nosed pliers may also come in handy.

If you have a means of producing electricity, or the grid hasn't gone down completely, a good-quality cordless drill can be a lifesaver, or at least keep you from early-onset carpal tunnel. Have at least one extra battery so you can charge one while using the other. Given that the weight difference between a twelve-volt and twenty-volt drill is fairly negligible, spring for the extra power. A comprehensive set of drill bits will also be helpful.

The prepper's basic toolbox for general repairs might consist of:

- ❏ hammers
- ❏ hand saws
- ❏ wrench sets (SAE and metric)
- ❏ pliers (various sizes)
- ❏ duct tape
- ❏ paracord

- ❏ screwdrivers (slotted, Phillips, and Torx)
- ❏ gas shutoff wrench
- ❏ flashlight/headlamp
- ❏ cordless drill with extra batteries
- ❏ drill bits (various sizes)
- ❏ tape measure

DEMOLITION TOOLS

It would not be unreasonable to assume any long-term disaster will bring with it the need for tearing down things as much as repairing them. For example, what if a tree lands on the back half of your shed? You're going to need to take apart what's left to see what you can salvage for a new one.

A few pry bars are a good place to start. Get a variety of sizes so you have a good representation of strength as well as ease of use in tight spots.

A framing hammer typically has a longer handle than a standard hammer, as well as a straight claw at the back of the head. These two factors make it ideal for some demo projects.

A come-along will be incredibly useful for moving large, heavy debris. For those not familiar, a come-along is basically a sort of ratcheting device, with a handle, straps, and hooks. You attach the come-along to a tree or other stable object. Then, a cable or strap runs from the come-along to the object you wish to move. By ratcheting the come-along, the cable or strap is pulled, moving the object.

Saws will also be handy when cutting lumber apart. Precision isn't generally that necessary with the type of demo work we'll be facing, so you might be able to get by with just a basic ripsaw or two. Use this checklist to help you gather the demolition tools you'll need:

- ❏ pry bars of various sizes
- ❏ hand saws
- ❏ strong rope
- ❏ come-alongs
- ❏ wheelbarrow
- ❏ rakes
- ❏ shovels
- ❏ tarps
- ❏ buckets
- ❏ framing hammer

CLEANING TOOLS

OK, granted, a mop and bucket probably aren't the first things that come to mind when we talk about tools. However, think about it like this: One of the reasons you'll need cleaning equipment is due to the repair and demo work you'll be doing. On top of that, of course, will be the general dirt and such that will build up just from living.

Start with rags and cleaning solutions like Mr. Clean. The goal might not be to create sparkling windows, but these cleaning products will help a great deal with keeping things somewhat sanitary. You're also going to find all sorts of uses for buckets. If you can find a local source for five-gallon pails, such as from delis and bakeries, pick up several.

Carpets are going to be troublesome as you won't be able to vacuum them. Rugs, of course, can be taken outside and beaten or shook. What you can do is invest in a manual carpet sweeper. These work surprisingly well, provided the nap of your carpet isn't too shaggy.

Brooms and dustpans are a given necessity. I prefer the old-fashioned corn brooms, but get whatever you personally like to use. Here's a helpful cleaning tool checklist:

- ❏ rags
- ❏ cleaning solution (such as Mr. Clean)
- ❏ vinegar
- ❏ bleach
- ❏ five-gallon buckets
- ❏ brooms
- ❏ dustpans

GARDEN TOOLS

Forget all about roto-tillers. Even if you have the fuel to operate one, odds are you're going to want to save the gas for something else. Instead, you can plan on digging, hoeing, weeding, and all that other fun stuff by hand.

At a bare minimum, you will want a shovel, a hard rake, and a few garden trowels. These will be enough to get you started in a basic garden. A wheelbarrow or garden cart will be very useful, perhaps more than you'd think. We have, at last count, four garden carts, and they are all constantly in use for various things, from transporting dirt from one location to another, to being a handy way of carrying all the garden tools at once.

A manual sod cutter will also be very good to have if you find yourself needing to break new ground for garden expansion. Rather than dig up the yard one shovelful at a time, these contraptions strip the sod off the soil. Don't forget to shake out all the dirt from the strips of sod before composting them. For one reason, it makes them much lighter and easier to carry. For another, the more dirt you keep in the garden, the better. Here's a helpful garden tool checklist:

- ❑ shovel
- ❑ hand trowels
- ❑ hoe
- ❑ small clippers
- ❑ sod cutter
- ❑ knee padding
- ❑ string (for training vine plants)
- ❑ tape measure or ruler (for spacing seeds)
- ❑ wheelbarrow or garden cart
- ❑ garbage bags
- ❑ manual carpet sweeper
- ❑ rake

FIREWOOD TOOLS

Whether you have a fireplace, a woodstove, or just a fire pit in the backyard, you are probably going to have to cut a fair amount of wood regularly. A chainsaw, while certainly a blessing, will only last as long as you have fuel for it. And even if you somehow had an unlimited fuel supply, you'd still have need for a few hand tools.

Start with a couple of good axes. They should be light enough for you to handle but heavy enough to do the job. A small hatchet isn't going to cut it, no pun intended.

A set of loppers as well as garden shears will work well for trimming off the smaller branches. While you could just swipe a large knife or machete at them, the loppers will be far safer for all concerned.

A bow saw is great for cutting medium-diameter logs to a manageable length. They work far better than just grabbing a crosscut or ripsaw from the workbench.

A sledgehammer and a wedge will help dramatically when it comes to splitting larger hunks of wood. I prefer using a sledge rather than a heavy axe just because I feel it is a safer approach. By the way, if you end up burying the wedge into the wood, the only real way you're going to get it out is to send another wedge down in there after it.

TOOL MAINTENANCE

You should also stock up on the equipment needed to keep your tools in good working condition. Files and whetstones for sharpening blades and saws. Extra handles for hammers and axes. Sure, it is possible to whittle new ones in a pinch, but spares aren't too expensive and will make things easier down the road.

Equally important, if not more so, is to learn the proper way to maintain the tools. Sharpening an axe is not something you can just pick up by reading a book. You really need to have someone show you how to do it and then practice it religiously every time you use the axe.

LIGHTING

Being able to shed some light on your subject will be very important, not only when working after sundown but also for protection. While candles and oil lamps are inexpensive, they aren't the most convenient or efficient way to provide light when working in confined spaces.

One relatively inexpensive investment is a set of solar-powered land-scape lights. Leave them outside all day long soaking up sunshine, then bring them in at night and stage them around the house for light. They aren't very bright, but they'll keep you from walking into walls or stubbing your toe on an end table.

Another solar option is the inflatable solar lantern, such as those made by LuminAID (LuminAID.com) or MPOWERD (MPOWERD.com). They have a small solar panel on the top that collects the energy. Then when it gets dark, you inflate them like a small pool toy and turn them on. They give off a fair amount of light and will last several hours on a single charge.

UVPaqlite is a company that specializes in glow-in-the-dark light solutions. They have a wide range of shapes and sizes to choose from. I can say they hold a light "charge" for quite a long time; these products are head and shoulders above the little glow-in-the-dark dinosaurs we played with as kids. But they provide only something of an ambient light source. They are great for marking a path, for example, but for reading or other tasks, maybe not so much.

As for battery-powered flashlights, this is another area where technology has made great leaps in recent years. LED lights are far brighter than the traditional incandescent bulbs of days gone by. Plus, they use much less energy, allowing your batteries to last longer. Avoid the cheap LED lights that you'll find on sale for under five bucks or so. They work great at first, but within just a few months, you'll notice problems with turning them on and keeping them lit, fresh batteries or no. Spend the extra few dollars and get something made to last. I highly recommend the Streamlight (Streamlight.com) brand.

Headlamps are another light option that I recommend. Being hands-free, they allow you to work much more efficiently. They aren't heavy or bulky, so they don't tax your neck if you wear them for extended periods of time.

Chemical lights, or ChemLights, are the glow sticks that you snap and shake to activate. The best ones on the planet are made by Cyalume (GetCyalume.com), with the brand name SnapLight. They come in a wide range of colors, but the illumination time does vary from one color to the next. The advantage is that these lights don't require electricity or batteries, they store well for long periods of time, and they're quite safe for kids. The downside, though, is that they are one-and-done, meaning that they are single-use. You can't turn them off and back on again. Still, they might make for a good backup option.

PROTECTIVE GEAR

Any time you use tools, you run the risk, however slight, of injury. A local radio station runs a contest every now and again where folks write in with their DIY mishaps, and the funniest or strangest ones get read on the air. I shouldn't be surprised, but I always am, at some of the outlandish things people have done while using tools. I know one guy personally who came very close to earning the nickname "Niner" by almost removing one of his toes when he decided to rinse off his feet with a pressure washer.

No matter how much of an expert you might be when it comes to working with tools, protective gear should be used whenever possible. This is even more critical when we're talking about a time in the future when running to the emergency room won't be on the list of options.

Proper eye protection is a must. Have on hand several pairs of safety glasses or goggles. Wear them any time there is even the slightest possible chance of something flying into your face while you're working on a project. If you think finding an emergency room physician will be tough after a collapse, try finding an eye doctor.

Heavy-duty work gloves will also be great to have. They will protect your hands from cuts, splinters, and scrapes, which could become infected later. I prefer all-leather gloves, but they do make some great gloves with other man-made materials.

Face masks are necessary when working with fumes or around smoke or sawdust. Look for the kind with the N95 rating, which can serve double duty to prevent airborne infections in the event of a pandemic.

Ear protection might not be quite as critical because you probably won't be working with all that much power equipment. But, even so, foam earplugs are very cheap and are advisable to have on hand, just in case. Use this checklist to help you gather your protective gear:

- ❑ heavy-duty work gloves
- ❑ safety glasses/goggles
- ❑ N95 dust masks
- ❑ knee pads
- ❑ steel-toe work boots
- ❑ ear protection (if power tools are still in use)

POWER GENERATION

Standard gas-powered generators will last only for so long. Either you'll run out of fuel or the generator will grow legs and walk away. After all, it is just about impossible to hide the fact that you are running a generator. They are loud, no two ways about it. Don't get me wrong; they are great for providing emergency power, and I do recommend preppers invest in them. Just don't look at them as a long-term solution to power generation.

Realistically, we can survive without electricity. I mean, humankind did just fine without it for thousands of years. Sure, it will be an adjustment, but so will everything else in the wake of a collapse.

That said, there are a few options you could consider for power generation. Solar is the first that comes to mind. You have two ways to go when it comes to solar power. The first is to purchase and install solar panels on or near your home. Doing so will likely require an electrician to install the proper wiring and other equipment. This is sort of a pricey endeavor to do properly, but there are various government programs that may help offset the cost. Plus, the advantage is everything is already in place, up and running, should the grid go down. With the proper size system, you'll be able to live much as you do today in terms of using electric lights and appliances.

The other route is to look at portable solar generators like those made by Goal Zero (GoalZero.com) and Jackery (Jackery.com). The nice thing about these products is they are portable. You can take them where you need them and not be tied to the structure of your home. Most of the companies producing these products have a range of devices available, from small units that will charge a cell phone to large systems that can power appliances.

There are also a few different products out there that will convert heat energy to electricity. The Biolite camp stove is one such product. Ridiculously simple to operate, it requires that you start a small fire in the stove. The heat energy powers an internal fan, which makes for an ultra-efficient fire. As the fire gets hotter, excess electrical energy produced is sent to a small USB port, allowing you to charge a cell phone or other USB-compatible device while you cook.

Keeping all that in mind, I still suggest you plan for life without electricity. Get used to the idea of not having a working refrigerator, a DVD player, or the internet. This way, if you do have a means to provide power, it is simply a bonus rather than a necessity.

COMMUNICATION TOOLS

Having the ability to acquire and share information is vitally important. Without it, you'll exist in something akin to a bubble, each day waiting to see if something is going to come along and pop it. The downside to communication tools is that they require power, typically from batteries. As long as you keep that in mind, and keep a stockpile of batteries set aside for this purpose, you'll be ahead of the game.

TWO-WAY RADIO

These have come a long way in recent years and are far better than the walkie-talkies you may have played with when you were a kid. However, don't believe the hype you'll see in the ads or on the packages. They may claim ranges of several miles, but the only way to achieve that is if there is absolutely nothing between you and the person on the other end. In reality, the effective range is greatly affected by obstacles like trees and buildings.

These radios come in two basic flavors: Family Radio Service (FRS) and General Mobile Radio Service (GMRS). These labels refer to the channels or frequencies the radios use. Broadcasting on the GMRS channels requires a license; the FRS channels do not. There are hybrid units available, which give you access to both GMRS and FRS frequencies.

Both FRS and GMRS radios basically operate on line-of-sight to the horizon, which in most places is about a mile or so. Again, though, the range is very much affected by what is around you. The range will be greater out in a field than it will in the middle of a city. Your best bet is to purchase a set of radios and play around with them. That's really the only way you'll know how far they reach in your particular area. Handheld units are going to have a shorter range than a base unit, simply because the base will have a larger antenna. The higher the antenna, the greater the broadcast range. What you might consider doing is investing in a base unit with a large antenna, then several handheld units you can distribute to group members as needed.

All in all, these two-way radios will work well for keeping members of your family or group in touch with one another. They may also allow for rapid communication between neighbors, which could be important if a threat is detected.

CITIZENS BAND RADIO

Most of us of a certain age remember *Smokey and the Bandit* or maybe *The Dukes of Hazzard*, complete with all sorts of jargon like, "I just saw a bear in a plain brown wrapper." While the popularity of CB radios has waned since the late 1970s and early 1980s, the equipment is still useful for short-range communication. And, no, you don't really need to know a "bear" is a law enforcement officer (typically a sheriff's deputy) and a "plain brown wrapper" means he's driving an unmarked squad car.

You're still only going to see effective ranges of maybe a few miles, but that's better than trying to stretch a string between two tin cans that far apart. CB radios come in handheld sizes, base units, and, of course, mobile units you can wire into a vehicle. Try to fight the urge to tell everyone you are "Rubber Duck" and are starting a convoy.

AMATEUR RADIO

Amateur (ham) radio is a great tool for communicating over long distances. It does require a license to broadcast, but the test isn't all that difficult if you take the time to study a bit. Ham radio is truly where it's at when it comes to gathering information. Ham operators have a long history of jumping in to assist in times of crisis, passing along information to those who need it.

If you want to get started with ham radio, I encourage you to seek out a local ham group in your area. Trust me, do a little digging online, and

I'll bet you a doughnut you find one within your county. I have met many ham operators over the years, and I have yet to encounter a single one who wasn't exceptionally helpful to those wishing to learn more. You'll also find that many ham operators already possess the necessary equipment to operate off the grid as needed.

Ham radio equipment, and the knowledge to use it effectively, will be greatly beneficial when it comes to communicating with other groups or towns. By establishing communication with them, you can work together to keep each other informed about potential threats as well as setting up trades and such.

SHORTWAVE RADIO

Think of ham radio as a subset of shortwave radio. Shortwave (SW) radio transmissions can travel the world over, which could be rather useful in a long-term survival situation in that you could find out information about your own country from impartial reporters. Quite often the news broadcasts from other countries contains information that isn't biased or skewed.

At the bare minimum, every prepper planning for some sort of collapse should invest in a decent shortwave radio receiver. Take the time to learn how to use it properly and earmark the frequencies that may be the most useful to you. Members of ham radio clubs may prove to be very helpful in that regard, as many of them will also be fans of SW radio listening.

CHAPTER 9

SURVIVING BOREDOM: ADDING ENTERTAINMENT TO SURVIVAL

Just after The Event, which is what many of us have taken to calling the day the power went out for good, we spent much of our time just trying to figure things out. Confusion and not a small amount of chaos reigned for perhaps longer than it really should have. But once things settled down and routines began to be established, many of us found ourselves with a fair amount of free time on our hands. In the evenings, after chores were done and it was too dark outside to do much of anything productive, we actually got bored. We'd been so accustomed to spending our down time watching TV or updating our social media pages, we just didn't know what to do with ourselves when those weren't options anymore.

We've now gotten to the point that many of us look forward to the time we have to get together and, in a way, get to know each other again. In talking to other families, we've heard about marathon sessions of Monopoly, sometimes lasting a few days or more. Others have done the same with card games, playing for matches or just owing each other on paper. Heck, there's even a weekly poker night that has been making the rounds of the neighborhood!

For us, we've gone through streaks of playing this or that game but lately have taken to having a family reading time. We've always had a pretty big library in our home so there are plenty of books to choose from. We take turns picking a book and go around the room, each of us reading a page or two out loud, then handing it off to the next person. It takes us a few evenings to get through an average book.

I guess if there is one good thing that has come out of this crisis, it is the general increase in the time we are spending together as a family. Of course, for far too many in our little community, there are a few empty seats around the table...

Make no mistake, surviving the aftermath of a societal collapse will involve a lot of hard work, quite possibly more work than you are used to doing on a daily basis. However, there will be down time. There will be a need to fight boredom. Some survivalists out there feel postdisaster life will be nothing more than a struggle from waking up at sunrise to collapsing from exhaustion at night. Personally, I look to examples from the past, to cultures such as the American pioneers in the 1800s, Native Americans, and even tribes from the most remote jungles. Each and every one of these groups had their own diversions to engage in once the work of the day was completed. I believe the same will hold true after a major event. At some point, daily routines will be established and, shortly thereafter, people will find themselves with time on their hands that needs to be filled.

See, here's the thing: Boredom can be extremely detrimental to survival thinking. If you sit and let the mind wander, doing little or nothing to engage the gray matter, it won't take long before despair might set in. Further, the brain should be treated as a muscle. If it isn't engaged in regular exercise, it will lose strength. If there is any time in your life you want your mind to be sharpest, it is when your survival depends on it, right?

Planning for entertainment needs might sound frivolous, I grant you that. But it is important to your psychological health to make time to relax a bit and have a laugh or three. Think of it as helping to keep in mind why you want to survive in the first place.

BOOKS

While I always advocate having hard copies of pertinent survival-related texts, here I'm talking about books you'd read for pleasure. I know not everyone is a reader in this sense, but many of us love to pass the time by visiting some exotic land via the magic of the printed page.

Fortunately, you can amass quite a substantial library for mere pennies. Library used-book sales as well as rummage sales are great places to start. I usually pay in the neighborhood of a buck for three or four paperbacks. As an admitted bibliophile, I've already accumulated far more books than I could ever hope to read in my lifetime. But that doesn't stop me from hitting the brakes whenever I see a used bookstore.

Everyone has different tastes when it comes to recreational reading, of course. Whether you personally prefer *Fifty Shades of Grey* or the latest doorstop by Stephen King, it is escapism you're after—something that can take your mind off the day-to-day struggles and maybe even give you something to look forward to in the evenings.

In addition to the books I would normally be interested in reading, I've also taken to collecting editions of literary classics. While the odds are pretty remote that the copies I've collected would be the only ones in the area to survive some sort of major calamity, I still feel better knowing they are there, just in case.

You might also consider setting aside inspirational works, particularly a copy of the Holy Bible or whatever religious text pertains to your own faith. For even casual believers, these works can provide a level of solace not found elsewhere.

If you are even an occasional reader, I'd suggest setting aside a box or two of books you find interesting. Keeping them in a plastic tote will go far toward preventing degradation from humidity and such. Don't forget to gather at least a few books suitable for kids. Even if you don't have young'uns in the house now, someone else might welcome a ratty old copy of *Green Eggs and Ham*.

BOARD GAMES

Another tried and true boredom reliever is games. While many homes likely have a few sitting in a back cabinet, it might be helpful to pull them out and at least make sure all the pieces are there. Further, while playing a round of Chutes and Ladders with your teenager might be fun for the sake of nostalgia, you might want to add a couple other games that are more age appropriate.

FARADAY CAGES

One of the most-feared disaster scenarios, at least among preppers and survivalists, is an electromagnetic pulse (EMP) knocking us back to the proverbial Stone Age. In theory, this would take out things like cell phones, mp3 players, tablets, laptops, and a myriad of other devices that we use on a daily basis to keep ourselves entertained.

As a practical matter, there's an awful lot we don't know for certain when it comes to what an EMP would or would not do. Sure, there are probably all sorts of studies and research done at government labs, but that data isn't available to common shlubs like you and I.

However, we do have an ace in the hole, so to speak. Dr. Arthur Bradley is a NASA engineer and one of the leading experts in the United States when it comes to EMP. He's written extensively on the subject. You can find him at DisasterPreparer.com.

A Faraday cage is basically a container that will protect electronic devices from an EMP. There are all sorts of ways to do this. Essentially, you want a container that has an outer layer of conductive material and an inner layer that's not conductive.

Here's one approach.

Take a copy paper box or other box with a separate lid and cover the entire outer surface with heavy-duty aluminum foil, including the tops of each side, folding the foil down into the box a bit. Also cover the lid and make sure the foil covers all of the inside lip of the lid.

Again, rummage sales can be great places to find board games on the cheap. Thrift stores sometimes have good selections as well. Just be sure to check the box contents to make sure everything is there. It can be difficult to play Monopoly if half the property cards are missing.

Avoid any games that require batteries, of course. Those AA and AAA batteries will likely be in short supply. The batteries you do have will need to be used for more important things.

Inside the box, cover the sides and the bottom with another layer of cardboard. Glue this all into place. For added protection, wrap each of your devices, such as walkie-talkies, tablets, or old cell phones, in bubble wrap or some other nonconductive material. Place them into the box, then close it up. It might not be absolutely necessary, but some people also use foil tape to seal the lid to the box. This should all serve to keep your electronics protected from an EMP.

A common question is whether the box or other Faraday cage needs to be grounded. Here's what Dr. Bradley has said about that:

There is a great deal of confusion regarding grounding of Faraday cages. Grounding a Faraday cage (i.e., connecting it to some Earth-referenced source of charge) has little effect on the field levels inside the box. Remember that "EMP bags" and other portable ad hoc Faraday cages provide excellent field reduction without any kind of ground connection. Grounding may help to keep the cage from re-radiating, but it is rarely worth the trouble. For large building-size structures, grounding plays other important roles, such as providing a path for lightning discharge and preventing possible shock hazards. The bottom line is that for all intents and purposes an ungrounded Faraday cage protects the contents from an EMP as well as a grounded one.

—Homemade Shielding (*Prepper Survival Guide* magazine #15, 2022)

CARDS AND DICE

Want to impress the kids? Show them it is indeed possible to play solitaire without electricity. In all seriousness, while you don't need to stock enough supplies to run a casino, there are thousands of games you can play with just a deck of cards or a few dice. What you might want to do is purchase a rule book or two to settle any arguments that may arise.

Unless you relish the thought of counting to fifty-two over and over, buy playing cards new rather than used. They are dirt cheap, so you aren't going to be saving a ton of money anyway. You could even purchase a few decks of cards that do double duty by having survival information or pictures of edible and medicinal plants printed on them. Sort of the prepper version of the nudie cards we used to sneak out of Dad's closet.

Dice are also very inexpensive and can come in handy with the aforementioned board games. A round of bar dice, anyone?

MUSIC

I'm neither a musician nor a singer. The description most apt when it comes to my vocal ability is "he can't carry a tune in a bucket." I do certainly appreciate music, though, and do not look forward to a day when listening to it is unavailable to me. One workable solution is to use an old cell phone as a portable music player and storage device. It can be easily charged using a small solar panel or similar setup. If the phone is equipped with an SD card expansion slot and you picked up a 32-gig SD card for it, you're talking a ballpark figure of about 10,000 songs that could be stored on it.

For those who have musicians in the family, ensuring they have the supplies they need for their instruments will be a very welcome addition to your overall preps. Guitar strings, drumsticks, and the like will probably be nearly impossible to find after a collapse. Who knows, there may come a time when forming your own version of the Partridge Family (hopefully sans bell bottoms) could pay off, if you barter your entertainment by charging admission fees consisting of canned goods and such. Even if the talents in the house don't extend quite that far, listening to your family members compose original works and perform old standbys can make for an enjoyable evening.

ARTS AND CRAFTS

Those of you with young children probably already appreciate the inherent value of construction paper, glue, and glitter. Such supplies can keep the kids out of your hair for hours, though crafting can lead to a fair amount of cleanup afterward. Those who have long since given up gluing macaroni to cardboard may still have a desire to get creative with scrapbooking.

Shop the back-to-school sales in late summer and stock up on all the necessary supplies—paper, glue, scissors, markers, colored pencils, tape, even staples and a stapler or two. Many of these items can be had for pennies on the dollar during those sales. Toss them all into a plastic bin, and they'll store just fine until you need them.

Being a writer, if I didn't have a notebook and a pen, I'd probably resort to scratching words in the dirt with a stick. Rather than let things get to that point, add several notebooks and some pens and pencils to your craft bin. Even if you don't consider yourself a writer, you might appreciate the ability to keep some sort of journal during the hard times. If nothing else, it can be somewhat psychologically cleansing to get your memories down on paper. Helpful hint: Though paper is fairly cheap, you can accumulate quite a bit for free if you work in or have access to an office-based business. Ask coworkers to save junk faxes and other paper that would otherwise just get tossed into recycling. You'd be surprised how quickly this adds up. In even a fairly small office, you can easily snap up about two reams a month or more. Sure, it is printed on one side, but who cares?

If you are an artist or like to dabble in art, stock up on the supplies you'll need. Paint, sketchpads, clay, all those materials will be nice to have on hand, and there's no way to predict when you might be able to get more. Of all the stores in town, I doubt Ben Franklin or Hobby Lobby will be high on the priority list to reopen after a disaster. Remember too that many crafts actually have practical value. Having the supplies and know-how to make a pot out of clay just might come in handy, for example. Hand-knit socks and mittens may also be quite welcome when the snow begins to fly.

The idea here is to plan ahead for ways to occupy your mind during the down times that are inevitable after a societal collapse. Relaxation and fun are good for the body, mind, and soul.

EDUCATION

Like entertainment, education might at first sound like something that should be pretty far down the prepper's priority list. Sure, I'd agree that things like food and water should take precedence. Remember, though, we're talking about events that could take years from which to recover.

It is important to plan ahead for educating children in the event their normal means of schooling becomes unavailable for the immediate future. First and foremost, an educated child will learn how to use logic and reasoning to come to a reasonable conclusion, rather than just relying upon snap judgment and emotions. Second, education will impart other skills to the student aside from those actually being taught. For example, time management and prioritizing are crucial life skills that will be learned through the process of juggling various assignments and such. Another example is problem solving. Few would argue against creative thinking not being a vital survival skill, right? By teaching students how to think outside the box, how to brainstorm, how to experiment to find what works, you dramatically increase their overall survival-skill toolbox.

This is one area of disaster planning where homeschoolers have a leg up on the rest of us. They've likely been at this for years already and have a good sense of what works and what doesn't. If the time comes when you feel it is necessary to begin educating the youth in your group, be sure to talk to those who have been there and done that.

You can plan ahead by availing yourself of the myriad homeschooling resources currently available. There are thousands of established groups for homeschooling families from coast to coast. Odds are pretty good there is at least one group in your area. If you don't know of any homeschooling parents yourself, do some digging online. Odds are pretty good there is at least one group in your area.

There are also roughly a gazillion websites devoted to homeschooling. Many of them offer study materials as well as complete course outlines. Just be sure you print out hard copies of what you decide to use.

Another source for educational materials, particularly textbooks and workbooks, is your local school district. Most schools receive new course materials every few years. When that happens, they will often offer up the used books for free to residents. Check with the local school principals to find out more information on the availability of course materials in your area.

CHAPTER 10

BARTER AND TRADE: NOT JUST FOR BASEBALL CARDS

As time went on, it became ever more apparent that those trusted greenbacks we were all accustomed to swapping were worth nothing more than tinder for campfires. The trading started small, with casual exchanges between neighbors. Instead of the stereotypical cup of sugar or flour, it was a few candles in exchange for charging a tablet with a generator. Before long, though, people began realizing the real worth of a can of beans or a couple batteries. Hard goods rapidly became the new currency.

A pair of new gloves, an all-but-forgotten Christmas present, might be worth two cans of stew on the "open market." A bar of soap, once found for free in any hotel room, is now worth at least a pair of gently used socks.

It isn't just trading goods for other material things either. A bag of good, homemade jerky will get your pants patched up nice and neat. A still-sealed bottle of generic brandy might fix a leak in your roof. Some people have even started little cottage industries as they became known as the go-to people for sewing and other skills. Mrs. Krueger, seventy-two years young and still going strong, will can your garden harvest in exchange for a percentage of the bounty and a promise to return the jars when they are empty.

There's been some talk of trying to come up with an actual system of currency that could be standardized in some way. After all, the whole idea behind the dollar was to simplify transactions. Great idea...on paper. The reality is, without some universally accepted standard of worth, we're probably better off deciding for ourselves what our goods and services are worth to us.

Putting aside the science of economics, the reality is that money is only worth what it will buy. If I'm hungry and have a hundred-dollar bill in my hand, the guy with the food decides how much it will purchase, if anything at all. After a societal collapse, odds are that portrait of Ben Franklin isn't going to get me squat.

Think about it like this: How often have you heard about people getting incredible deals at rummage sales simply because the seller had little idea of what the item was really worth? Or occasionally the deal is great because the item just isn't worth much to the seller. For example, I stopped at a garage sale some years ago and found a large backpack filled to the brim with survival gear like rope, camouflage netting, camp cookware, and even some fishing supplies. The seller commented that it had belonged to an old roommate who had stiffed him for some rent. His asking price? A whopping five bucks. The seller had no interest in the gear; he just wanted it gone. I was all too happy to oblige.

Barter and trade work on a similar principle. An item is worth only what it will bring in trade. High-dollar merchandise today, such as TVs, tablet computers, and fancy coffee makers, will be pretty much worthless in a world without reliable electricity. On the other hand, wool blankets (ugly patterns or not), heavy-duty gloves, and strike-anywhere matches will likely bring premium prices.

BARTER GOODS AREN'T A PRIORITY

The concept of barter and trade is immensely popular among preppers and survivalists. This isn't necessarily a bad idea, sort of a way of hedging your bets. But, based on the prevalence of the topic, I fear that some people place far more importance on this area of prepping than is perhaps prudent.

Successful bartering, particularly in some sort of post-collapse environment, will be predicated upon three things coming together:

1. You have something someone else wants/needs.

2. That same person has something you want/need.

3. You're able to connect with one another.

In the here and now, that's not difficult to pull off. There are any number of websites where you can post something you have available and entertain offers at your convenience. If the grid is down and social media gone along with it (saints be praised and sing Hallelujah), it might be a bit more difficult to arrange. Let's say you're in dire need of, I don't know, maybe decent plastic to replace a broken window pane. How will you find out whether someone in your area has it and might be interested in a trade?

Bartering isn't an inherently bad idea. I'm just saying that it might be best to look at it as a secondary option rather than a primary plan. With that in mind, if you have thoughts of trading with people in your area, you might consider laying that groundwork now. Showing up at their door out of the blue five weeks into a collapse and asking if they have XYZ to trade might not sit well, not if you don't have at least some sort of relationship with them. Hell, if you aren't well known to them, you might not even make it to their front door.

I'm not suggesting you tell them that you think the world is perhaps just weeks away from falling apart so you want to establish trading rights ahead of time. Instead, just try to work out a few simple trades every now and again so you're a familiar face. If they have chickens and you raise bees, maybe see if they're willing to trade eggs for honey.

The entire purpose behind disaster preparedness is to have what you need when you need it, right? While picking up a few extras here and there, just in case, isn't a bad idea, planning to be some sort of post-apocalyptic wheeler-and-dealer is probably a bad approach. Concentrate on stocking the things you'll likely need and add in barter goods when it makes sense to do so, rather than making that a primary focus.

STOCKPILING BARTER GOODS

If you are prepping for a calamity that will have long-term effects, it is wise to give thought to storing items specifically to be used for barter if your current form of currency bottoms out.

When trying to determine which items make for good candidates for future bartering, I have a few rules I try to follow.

PREPPER'S TOP TEN BARTER ITEMS

1. Alcohol/booze
2. Tobacco
3. Salt
4. Sugar/honey
5. Coffee/tea
6. Fresh vegetables/fruit
7. Heirloom seeds
8. Toiletries (toothpaste, soap, deodorant, etc.)
9. Toilet paper
10. Chocolate

First, the item must be inexpensive now. I feel it makes absolutely no sense to spend a ton of money stockpiling things that may or may not be needed for trading. Of course, this rule is also somewhat relative in that what I feel is expensive might not seem that pricey to someone else.

Second, the item must store well long-term. Nothing perishable or fragile, for example. You want to focus on things that you can put on a back shelf in a closet and forget about until they are needed.

Third and perhaps most important, the item should have value to you. By that, I mean the item must have some use to you in the event that the opportunity to trade it never materializes. Think of stocking up on barter goods as storing a little bit extra of some things you'd already want to have on hand.

Naturally, there are exceptions to these rules, as we'll talk about shortly. But, in general, if you follow the above guidelines you should be just fine.

POTENTIAL BARTER ITEMS

Now, this is a topic that usually generates a fair amount of discussion (read: argument) on the various survival-related social media sites. What one guy or gal thinks is a good item to stockpile, someone else says is worthless or stupid, if they don't use more colorful language. The fact is, no one knows for certain which particular items will be the most useful for potential trading. In a sense, you are having to gamble a bit. You are trying to anticipate a future need and hedge against it.

All that said, there are several things that are very likely to have tremendous value after a societal collapse.

Matches, particularly the strike-anywhere kind, are very cheap and easy to store. Just keep them cool and dry, and they'll last quite a while. What is particularly nice about using matches for barter is the ability to tailor the amount to the trade. A dozen matches might be worth a candle or two, while a box of them could get you several cans of food. I suggest storing matches in their original boxes, sealed in zip-top plastic bags or even vacuum-sealed plastic.

BARTERING WITH BULLETS IS A BAD IDEA!

There are some people who argue, quite vehemently, that ammunition, particularly .22LR, will be used as ersatz currency in a postdisaster world. To my way of thinking, this is folly at best. On the one hand, I see little issue with trading a few bullets to a trusted neighbor. But, on the other hand, who's to say the person to whom you give the bullets won't want to return them to you at a high velocity? Never, ever, trade ammunition or weapons!

Basic **fishing gear** is very inexpensive. Hooks, line, sinkers, bobbers, all can be had on the cheap in any sporting goods department. Rods and reels can be a bit more expensive, but if you hunt around rummage sales and such, you'll find them for pennies on the dollar. As the saying goes, teach a man how to fish...

Various **toiletries**, such as toothbrushes, toothpaste, soap, and shampoo, will be very desirable within a few months of the collapse. Into this category would also fall "luxuries" like **lip balm** and **hand lotion**. It isn't always about pure survival. Anything that will help people feel human again will be of value.

There are also a few things that many people will likely not have thought to stockpile, even though they use them on a very regular basis. These include **feminine hygiene products**. While there are alternatives, such as reusable pads made from old T-shirts and the like, I think most women would be more comfortable using the products they've become accustomed to using. **Condoms** and other birth control methods will also be of value. No matter how bad the circumstances, people will always find a way to hook up. If pregnancy can be avoided until life returns to normal, all the better.

Given that options for buying new clothing will be somewhere between slim and none, new **socks** may well be seen as quite a prize. Along these same lines are **needles**, **thread**, **patches**, and **bolts of cloth**. While not many people may be interested in cobbling together their own shirts from loose material, makeshift patches for shirts are easily made.

Even if you can't offer medical advice or treatment, you might consider stocking up on **pain relievers** like ibuprofen or acetaminophen. These medications are very inexpensive currently and could bring high prices when they are no longer easily available. **Multivitamins** will also be welcome as diets might not be quite as varied as they are now, leading to nutritional deficiencies. Even simple **caffeine pills** will have great value to those who no longer have easy access to coffee or tea.

Then, we have the vices. **Tobacco**, **alcohol**, **candy**, and **coffee** will be highly prized. There is no need to go out and spend a ton of dough on the high-dollar top-shelf liquor either. Even the cheapest rotgut will find a home at some point. For smokers, stock up on bags of loose tobacco and rolling papers rather than packs of cigarettes. Toss the bags in your freezer until the time comes when you lose power and eventually need to trade it. Coffee could be stored as raw beans, ready for roasting, or as jars of instant. I know, I know, you Starbucks junkies cringe at the thought of crystallized caffeine. But push come to shove, you'll line up for just a smell of that instant coffee once you're forced to go without your normal java.

Just about any food item will have value, but a few particular ones might prove to be a rarity and therefore command higher prices. **Salt** is dirt cheap right now, but when it is no longer available at the local grocery, people will realize how important it is. Students of history know how valuable salt has been in the past. At various times, it was even used as payment for troops and such. **Sugar** will also be prized, as will **honey**. Anything that will help add variety to the diet will be welcome, even **powdered drink mixes**.

Heirloom seeds are something of a long-term investment. At the beginning of a crisis they may not be seen as valuable, but the longer it goes on, the more people will realize their importance. I suggest keeping them in their original packaging to help prove the seeds are going to grow into what you say they will. Many people can't tell the difference between the seeds of a tomato versus those of a gourd. To store them for the long haul, you just need to keep them cool and dry. We've kept seeds in simple paper envelopes for years without any problems with germination.

While I'd consider them to be more high-ticket items than casual trades, **hand tools**, like hammers, saws, wrenches, and pliers, will be needed by many people who are suddenly finding themselves having to do repairs on their own. You can find them now somewhat cheap at rummage sales and some thrift stores. However, I'd avoid buying any at discount stores or, *shudder*, dollar stores. There is a reason tools found in those places are so cheap, and it isn't because of the generosity of the retailer.

In addition to tools like hammers and wrenches, don't forget **gardening tools**. Shovels, trowels, and such will be needed by people who have never had to break ground before. For many such tools, you might be better off setting up some sort of rental agreements rather than trading them outright. While this might not always be feasible, it is something to consider.

MAKING A LIVING

Material goods aren't the only things that will be traded. Bartering one's services is also bound to be an important part of the postcollapse economy. Many skill sets will quite naturally lend themselves to cottage industries of a sort. Occupations like computer programmer, advertising executive, and cashier will fall to the wayside. Most, if not all, businesses will probably close up, with the possible exception of smaller shops that convert into trading posts of a sort. While people will be spending much more time than they do currently on just surviving, many will gradually develop their own home businesses, filling some sort of need within the community at large. By planning ahead, you can pick your niche, so to speak.

It should go without saying that any kind of **medical skills** will be highly valued. That could mean having experience as a doctor or nurse or perhaps an emergency medical technician (EMT) or paramedic. If you have the opportunity to gain skills and experience in the medical field, I'd highly encourage you to do so. Same goes for dental care. Given how closely dental health is tied to overall well-being, having the ability to effectively treat mouth infections and such will be quite a boon to your family and neighbors. Into this category would also fall those who

167

have experience and skills with using wild medicinals to treat medical issues. In some postcollapse communities, the only available medical treatments might be those using plants foraged and/or garden grown.

Trades like **plumbing**, **carpentry**, and **electrical work** will also be sought after. Knowing how to properly wire up a generator or build a shelter for it will benefit not only you and your family but those around you. Should a time come that fire departments cease responding, the last thing you want is for your neighbor's house to catch fire because they didn't know how to properly install a transfer switch. When it comes to fashioning defensive constructions for your community, those who are familiar with the building trades will be of great benefit.

Along those same lines would be **small engine repair** and other wrench-turning skills. Though we can't possibly know what the future will bring, there may still be opportunities for people who know how to get a motor running again. If the thought of a community relying upon go-karts powered by old lawn mower engines sounds ridiculous to you, well, I'd say you lack imagination.

Can you imagine the worth of well-made knitted socks or mittens? Much of the clothing sold today is made of inferior materials and is poorly constructed, with an eye toward fashion rather than functionality. Those with skills in **sewing**, **knitting**, and the like will have plenty to occupy their hands within just a few months of the collapse.

If there is only one person who won't ever go hungry, it will be the guy or gal who can provide the hooch. **Home brewing** has become rather common today, and the equipment for doing so is easy to find. This isn't a skill that can be learned overnight, though, and takes time to perfect. Whether through craft beers, wine, or even moonshine, people will always seek a release, an escape, from their day-to-day existence.

There is also a litany of what we often refer to as **homesteading skills**. Many of these have become somewhat popular again, such as soap making and candle making. See if there are any "living museums" in your area and, if so, visit them. These are places where you can observe how people truly lived back in the day, with museum employees actually performing the work in front of you. One such place is found in Eagle, Wisconsin, aptly named Old World Wisconsin. It consists of several settlements, most with small farms and such. Strolling through one of these museums for an afternoon will give you great insight into just what life may be like after a societal collapse.

Don't overlook the possibility of entertainers eking out some sort of living. Those with skill in **music**, **acting**, or **comedy** may be able to provide much-needed distraction. This was actually a plot device in David Brin's novel *The Postman* and has, I think, some validity. Keep in mind that during the Great Depression, people flocked to the cinema, spending hard-earned money just to be whisked away for a couple hours.

Of course, with any of these hobbies-turned-occupations, it is important to have all the required supplies and gear stockpiled for future use. Stock up as much as you can, bearing in mind that getting more necessary supplies may one day be difficult, if not impossible.

THREE RULES FOR BARTERING

If what we suspect holds true and bartering becomes a part of routine life in a postcollapse world, you would do well to heed a few general rules.

1. Be fair in all transactions. Do not go into a trade with the intention of trying to get one over on the other person. You may end up having to deal with them again down the road, and it will be much better if they remember you as someone who did right by them. Ideally, both parties involved in each trade will think they got the better end of the deal.

2. Don't trade away something you can't afford to lose. I think many of us have probably been in a tight spot before and done something we

later regret. I once sold a very nice compound bow for pennies on the dollar at a rummage sale. Why? We were flat broke and desperately needed cash. So, I let it go for a song. While we put the money to good use, buying some much-needed groceries, to this day I wish I'd have sold something else. Fortunately, we live in a day and age when you can conceivably go to a store and purchase a replacement. But when there aren't any stores operating anymore, you won't have that luxury.

3. Avoid what we might call "sweetheart" deals. These are situations where you might offer an extremely good deal to someone, typically because they are a good friend or neighbor. The problem with doing so is people tend to talk, and if you don't offer the same sort of deal to someone else, they could get upset. While today that might not be a big concern, if that person were the only one around offering fresh eggs, you might find yourself painted into a corner.

¤ ¤ ¤ ¤

In the aftermath of a major event, I can easily see small, open-air markets cropping up here and there. Looking very much like current flea markets, these will provide opportunities for people to trade this for that in a relatively safe environment. In fact, some community leaders might even encourage the development of such markets. Doing so would not only foster commerce of a sort but also provide a means of fellowship among the community members.

CHAPTER 11

COMMUNITY SURVIVAL PLANNING: IT TAKES A VILLAGE

Many of us have been attending weekly community meetings, sort of like old-fashioned town hall meetings, actually. We're making plans for the future as well as addressing more immediate problems. There's talk of planting spring gardens at a couple of the parks. Quite a few people have seed packets, though a lot of them are kind of old so we're not sure how many will germinate. Still, it is good that we're looking ahead. Wish we'd done that a long time ago.

Early on, it was decided that what was left in the supermarket and the convenience stores would be taken and kept at the high school. Those who had canning equipment jumped right in to help preserve the perishable stuff. Guards were put in place to keep out looters and thieves. They then started slowly doling it out to those in need. Every week, it seems like more and more people are showing up and standing in line. But we've been told that between those supplies and a few other sources, there should be enough food for us to survive until spring. Of course, that's also with a heavy helping of deer and other game that we're hoping to harvest through the winter.

Almost all of us, those who are physically able anyway, have jobs within the community now. I put in a few shifts a week at one of the roadblocks we set up along the town's perimeter. I've also been helping out at the school with cooking and serving meals. None of us collect anything like a paycheck, of course. I guess we look at it as just part of the deal. The community will live, or die, based on our support.

It saddens me greatly that it took a giant disaster like this to finally open our eyes, to get us to realize that we need to be human to each other for us to all survive.

I've always been a big proponent of community survival planning. When it comes to surviving a long-term crisis, the lone wolves just won't make it, for the most part. I've had the opportunity to get to know many survival experts over the years. Guys and gals who could go out into the woods with nothing more than a pocket knife and come out a month later having actually gained fifteen pounds and riding a bike they fashioned out of willow branches and honey badger carcasses. Every single one of them, when asked, would tell you that living off the land for extended periods of time is their backup plan, not their primary intention, should a crisis come to pass.

WHAT IS A COMMUNITY?

I suppose we should take a moment to clarify the term "community." For the purposes of our discussion, it refers to a group of people who, whether by accident or design, are all living within a set boundary after a disaster. A community could be a village or a town of several thousand people. It could also be a small neighborhood within a larger city or perhaps a semirural subdivision at the outskirts of a town. The community might even be a group of individuals who have created an off-site survival retreat and have been working toward this specific goal for years.

It is impossible to define or quantify the term "community" in terms of population figures, at least for our purposes. The overriding principle at work here is that a group of people will stand a much better chance at long-term survival than the lone individual.

BENEFITS AND CHALLENGES OF COMMUNITY-BASED SURVIVAL

The first and foremost advantage of community-based survival is the quantity and diversity of supplies available within the community. We'll talk more about community assets in a bit, but do some quick mental calculations: How many restaurants, schools, taverns, convenience stores, and supermarkets are there in your town? Each of those will have a fair supply of food on hand, as a matter of course. If the owners of such businesses were to chip in to some sort of community storage area, those supplies could go a long way toward keeping people fed for a while.

There is also definite safety in numbers. A group of people stand a much better chance of setting up adequate defenses than just one or two individuals. You can set up rotating shifts for lookouts, for example. Plus, many hands make for light work and all that.

PLANNED SURVIVAL GROUPS

In recent years, there has been a dramatic rise in the number of intentional survival groups in the United States and elsewhere. The idea behind them is to gather a group of people of similar mindset together ahead of time, forming a cohesive body that works together to plan for future survival. Some are quite advanced in their planning, having secured real estate, built structures, and stockpiled ample supplies. Other groups are more informal, more akin to a hunting club, where the members get together only once in a while but have agreed to help each other should the need arise.

These groups go by many names—retreat groups, mutual aid groups (MAGs), intentional communities. On the whole, they are generally a great idea. Being an active member of a group working toward long-term survival can be educational and beneficial for you and your family. However, most established groups aren't looking for strangers to sign up. In fact, the majority of groups consist of people who have known each other for many years and enjoy the level of trust only a lifetime of familiarity can bring.

With that in mind, you might consider starting your own group rather than trying to seek out an established one to join. There is a lot more to starting a group than just buying a spot of land and positioning a few supplies on it.

You also have diversity in available skill sets. As much as we'd like to pretend or fantasize to the contrary, it is mighty difficult for one person or even a small family to possess all the potentially necessary skills for long-term survival. But within an entire community, odds are definitely in your favor that you'll have at least a few, if not several, medical professionals, quite a number of gardeners, probably several skilled tradespeople, all within the population. Add in the police officers, hunters, and firearm enthusiasts, and you have the makings for a decent defensive force.

Of course, cooperating at a community level isn't all sunshine and rainbows. A town will have a lot more mouths to feed than just a small family. There will also be many disparate personalities that need to be turned around and focused toward a common goal. Leadership issues may crop up from time to time.

Also, to be frank, not every person in town is likely to be a model citizen. In any group of significant size, there is going to be a percentage of liars, thieves, layabouts, chronic alcoholics or drug abusers, and other not-so-desirable types. That percentage will vary, of course, but it will always be there.

Another problem is many communities are still somewhat behind the times, so to speak, with disaster planning. Sure, they might post a few public service announcements about having an emergency kit in the car, or have leaflets available that discuss FEMA's guidelines on emergency preparedness. But, when it comes to long-term stuff, many towns and villages, not to mention the larger cities, just don't discuss the topic all that much, if at all.

And that, dear reader, is where you come in. While the "powers that be" might not be too worried about an EMP taking down the grid, you can certainly do your own homework and be in a position to assist should such an event take place. What follows is based on what we might call the "Survival Community Ideal." Bear in mind that reality is often far from ideal, and some of the following suggestions might not be feasible in your own situation. But, even so, it is important to give serious thought to each so you are better prepared to help your own community survive whatever might come down the road.

ROLES WITHIN THE COMMUNITY

For a community to survive, even thrive, during a long-term crisis, there are several different roles that will need to be fulfilled. Think of them as jobs, if that makes it easier to imagine. Any organized group of survivors will have the same needs that must be filled. Of course, smaller groups may find their members wearing multiple hats.

LEADERSHIP

In order for a group or community to be successful, it will require leadership. In the immediate aftermath of a disaster, this role may be filled by default by those currently occupying elected positions—mayor, alderman, city administrator, etc. Certainly the chief of police will be involved, possibly the fire chief as well. This is not an inherently bad thing. Provided the officials aren't brand-new, they should already possess experience with interpersonal conflict resolution and people management, both of which are skill sets critical to a successful transition from the status quo today to a very different tomorrow.

LOGISTICS

Put simply, logistics refers to coordinating an operation or series of events involving many people and/or a range of supplies. In other words, where leaders will be able to make decisions as to *what* needs to happen, those in the logistics area are the ones with experience in *how* to make it happen. Don't think of these people as if they are simply middle-management types, as that is far from the case. These folks are able to make a concrete plan to get something accomplished and know how to leverage available resources. They not only know how to keep track of supplies, they have a talent for predicting future needs and working to satisfy them.

SECURITY

Actually a few different elements fall under the security umbrella. First, and most obviously, you have those providing protection against threats coming from outside the community. At any given time, there may be people who want what your community has, whether that be food, water, supplies, or even women. Related to this, you may find a need to have groups of people from your community venture outside, perhaps to scavenge or maybe just to keep an eye on the world immediately around you. We'll call these "scouting missions." Any time you send scouts out, they will need to be protected. Finally, you will need to have some means of enforcing the rules or laws within the community. Despite what anarchists might dream of, some form of law and order will need to be in place.

MEDICAL

Another critical role within the community is health care. Of course, the ideal would be having a fully equipped and staffed hospital. However, that's probably not going to be the case for the majority of communities, and, as a result, they will have to make do with what they have. Anyone within the community known to have any sort of medical experience should be tapped for this group. These would include:

- doctors
- nurses
- dentists
- dental assistants
- emergency medical technicians (EMTs)
- paramedics

- those certified in first aid, such as Boy Scouts or Red Cross volunteers

FOOD PRODUCTION

Any community will require sustenance. While it would be the height of great fortune to have each member of the group already set up with their own sustainable food supply, that probably won't be the case. If I had to guess, I'd say the average family probably has enough food in their home to last them maybe a week at best. As we'll talk about shortly, there are many sources of food already in place within the typical community. However, those sources won't last forever, and plans will need to be made as soon as possible for getting gardens in the ground. What I envision is not only having community members build their own home gardens but also setting up community plots. These would not only provide food for those who lack garden space, such as apartment dwellers, but also augment the overall community food storage.

GRUNT LABOR

For those who lack the skills to fill one of the above roles, plenty of work will still be available—disaster cleanup, for example. In just about any societal collapse scenario that comes to mind, there will likely be widespread damage. Perhaps not as a direct result of the disaster but almost certainly from rioters and looters if nothing else. Hands and backs will also be needed for cutting firewood, distributing supplies, and perhaps even providing some level of emergency services like firefighting. Rest assured, even someone with no readily apparent survival skills will have a role to play within the community.

COMMUNITY ASSET ASSESSMENT

As noted earlier, most community leaders, if they think or talk at all about disaster planning, focus primarily on the short-term emergencies that are somewhat common. Few, if any, give much thought to the sorts of long-term disasters that are our focus here. Therefore, I suggest you do some planning for them. Grab a pen and some paper and start making lists of assets within the community. The overall idea here is to get a handle on what might be available to the community if the worst were to happen.

FOOD AND WATER

There are probably dozens of places within your own community where large amounts of food, particularly items suited for long-term storage (such as canned goods), are kept just as a matter of routine business.

- restaurants
- taverns
- convenience stores
- supermarkets
- discount retailers
- school cafeterias

As soon as it becomes evident this is a long-term event, measures should be taken to protect these assets from looters. While there may not be much left at some of the larger stores, given they are the easy targets, many people will probably overlook the smaller retail outlets and almost certainly schools. Taverns and bars will also be hard hit, but looters may have ignored the food in their rush to get at the beer and booze. If there are businesses in town that have their own cafeterias, these should also be included in this category.

Something else to consider are vending machines that might have survived the initial onslaught. Sure, chips and candy bars aren't exactly nutritious fare, but many vending machines today actually have semihealthy offerings such as granola bars and nuts. While you're thinking along these lines, bear in mind that many workers keep stashes of food at their desks. Not a lot, mind you, but it all adds up. Let's say the office building has seven floors and fifteen workstations or cubicles per floor—that's over a hundred possibilities for food in just one building.

Those same retail outlets and vending machines will also have quantities of bottled water available, as well as other beverages. Keep in mind that while soft drinks and the like aren't nearly as healthy as plain water, they can still slake thirst in the short term. However, lest I be called on the carpet for neglecting to mention it, many sodas and other canned or bottled beverages may actually work against the body in the long term. Caffeine, in particular, is a diuretic, meaning it makes you pee more often.

You should also make note of any local natural bodies of water—rivers, lakes, ponds, and streams. While such water will need to be filtered

SEIZING PRIVATE ASSETS

As we go forward in this section, you'll notice I've sometimes listed privately owned businesses as assets that might be used for public welfare. While I have mixed feelings about this approach, I do believe it is worth considering. Certainly, if the owners of such businesses are readily available, they should be consulted and their permission sought before outright seizures take place. But with many of the big-box retailers out there, the entities owning that merchandise could very well have ceased to exist in the event of a collapse.

I would suggest that if such measures are taken, a detailed accounting of the resources seized should be made whenever realistically possible. When the time comes that things return to some semblance of normalcy, those concerned could then be reimbursed in some way.

and disinfected, it would not be overly difficult to develop a system for doing so on an ongoing basis for community residents.

MEDICAL SUPPLIES

In addition to the usual suspects such as Walmart and Walgreens, as well as medical clinics, there are several other places you'll find at least basic first aid gear. While you're at the schools checking the cafeterias, be sure to stop at the nurses' offices, where you're sure to find bandages and other supplies. Most factories and other businesses will also have first aid kits socked away.

As quickly as possible, measures should be taken to secure any and all pharmacies within the community. Even if they have been looted, odds are very good that the thieves took the narcotics while leaving the healing drugs behind. Other locations where drugs and supplies might be found would include medical clinics and dental offices. The latter in particular might prove to be especially useful, given the anesthetics and other medications likely to be present.

EMERGENCY SHELTERS

Emergency housing is one thing community leaders probably have a good handle on, but it pays to be prepared anyway. If the disaster ends up destroying large numbers of homes, survivors will be displaced and in need of shelter, perhaps for some time to come. Give thought to where these folks could be housed. Many churches often offer emergency shelter for the homeless, particularly during cold winter months, but their space is usually severely limited. You need to think bigger.

School gymnasiums are one common option. If there aren't enough cots to go around, most schools have an abundance of mats that could be used.

Assuming there are vacancies at local apartment buildings as well as hotels, the owners of such might be willing to allow refugees to stay for a while, at least until other arrangements can be made. Even if the actual owners are from out of town and unreachable, a property manager is likely to be on site.

While it might be impossible to predict ahead of time, another possibility worth noting is that families might be willing to take in one or two extra people, provided that enough food and supplies are available for them. This is particularly true in the case of children whose parents have perished or were out of town when the disaster hit. If this option were to be implemented, I'd suggest involving whatever remains of local law enforcement, consulting them to ensure there are no known sex offenders already residing in the "foster" homes.

LIBRARIES

While those under the age of, say, thirty might not believe this, before the internet became commonplace, we used to have to visit actual buildings to look up information. Thankfully, many of those buildings still exist and are packed full of knowledge to this day.

Should the time come when we're no longer able to simply Google up the sum total of humankind's knowledge, libraries will have to pinch hit. That's where you'll be able to find necessary information on a range of useful topics, from the proper spacing of turnip seedlings to how to diagnose Lyme disease.

LAND TO REPURPOSE

Earlier I mentioned the idea of setting up a system of food production within the community after a disaster. Most communities have large tracts of land that could be repurposed as gardens or as areas for raising animals. Examples include parks and golf courses, both of which will have large open areas suitable for farming. Many schools also have large areas of flat land that could be used. The soil might not be ideal, but with amendments such as peat moss and fertilizer liberated from hardware stores and garden shops, it could be easily improved.

Of course, even small areas of land should be used. The courtyards of condo developments and backyards of apartment buildings should be sown and planted. Every little bit helps. Residents of the community should be encouraged to plant their own gardens as well, with the idea being any excess would be donated to the community's food storage. However, and let me be very clear on this, this sort of arrangement

RESEARCHING EXISTING EMERGENCY PLANS

Shortly after 9/11, the Department of Homeland Security, FEMA, and other agencies began to encourage counties throughout the United States to formulate their own emergency plans in the event of disasters. They made grants available to finance such endeavors, and most counties took them up on the offer. As a result, the vast majority of counties have appointed at least one individual to be the emergency coordinator. In my experience, most of these folks are members of the county sheriff's department. On top of that, many municipalities have done the same and created their own emergency plans that would work in conjunction with those of the county.

The plans that were drawn up are a matter of public record. As a result, you, as a citizen, have every right to see them, and even get copies of those plans. I noted earlier that most of these emergency planners aren't thinking in terms of true "end of the world as we know it" scenarios, so don't expect to see a whole lot of information like we're covering here. But it pays to be informed, so I highly encourage you to seek out the emergency coordinators at the county and local levels, and obtain copies of the plans they have devised. They may have thought of things you might have overlooked. Plus, reading through those plans will give you some great insight into what to expect (or not to expect) from local government agencies.

should not be perceived as taxation in any way, shape, or form. Strictly voluntary is the way to go.

SECURITY ISSUES

Obtain a map showing the area of your community; something that shows a street-level view would be best. Do your homework and determine every single access point to the community. Every highway, every back road, even well-known hiking trails or bike paths that cross into the community should be noted. These access points are where you can expect to see refugees coming through. Consequently, these are the places where you will want to have guards or roadblocks placed to prevent unknown individuals from entering the area.

It would probably be nigh impossible to fence off the entire community. But luckily, human beings are generally somewhat lazy. Rather than hike through miles of unknown forest and fields, they will walk the roads and highways. Therefore, it is those areas that should be of most concern and that deserve the most attention.

COMMUNITY ORGANIZATION AND LEADERSHIP

There are many ways to organize and lead a postcollapse community. At one end of the spectrum, you might have a communal sort of arrangement, with every single person sharing the same level of responsibility and no actual ownership of anything. At the other end, you might have a single ruler, one guy or gal who calls all the shots and makes all the rules, and who is served by the members of the community.

As with most things in life, the ideal lies somewhere between the extremes. Most average citizens will chafe against an all-mighty ruler. And there's a reason why you don't see very many "peace and love" communes dotting the landscape today.

What I suggest is forming a committee that will be placed in charge of the day-to-day operations of the community. This committee should consist of a representative from each of the major work groups—security, food production, medical, and logistics. You may also wish to include one or two additional people drawn from the general population. This committee would work together to make any necessary decisions and create plans for the community.

In this approach, no single person is considered more important than another. While the members of the committee are seen as being "in charge" of the group as a whole, no specific individual reigns supreme. Further, each of the work groups within the community is represented and has a voice in the decision-making process.

Depending upon the circumstances, you could also consider allowing the community members to each have a vote in at least some decisions that need to be made. This might prove to be a laborious process if the community is fairly large, but people did just fine with this approach for decades before computers became commonplace.

The committee may also be placed in charge of handling the community disputes that will inevitably arise. Whether you task the committee with this or appoint some other individual or group, it is important to have some means of resolving grievances among community members. While one would hope individuals could handle such things on their own, history has shown the need for an impartial person or group to handle some of these decisions.

MAKING AND ENFORCING COMMUNITY LAWS

While many of the laws on the books will likely continue to stand, for convenience if nothing else, some will need to be changed and others created anew. For example, stealing an apple from the grocery store today will probably net you nothing more than a ticket for shoplifting. You'd pay a small fine and be on your way. Stealing food in a postcollapse world, though, might be considered a capital offense. Reason being, stealing food that cannot be easily replaced could result in one or more people starving.

Further, the penalties currently enforced today might not be feasible. How would you go about imprisoning someone for a few months, let alone a year or more? How could you levy a fine when money has no real value any longer? While the first inclination might be to banish those who are found guilty of committing serious crimes, that punishment might not end up being in the community's best interests. Should you decide to remove someone from the community and cut them loose outside the gates, as it were, what you've done is to take someone who knows the inner workings of the community intimately and place them in a position where they can reveal that information to those who would do your community harm. In fact, the removed individual might even feel rather motivated to do exactly that.

Is capital punishment the solution? I don't know; maybe. Certainly for the most egregious crimes—rape, murder, child molestation—something needs to be done to ensure the individual doesn't do it again. Remember too that punishment serves as a deterrent to those who might consider committing similar crimes. Therefore, while it sounds barbaric, perhaps a viable solution might be some form of corporal punishment.

Another option to consider would be forced labor in the fields or something like that. However, you then run the risk of demoralizing the workers already doing such tasks, if they feel their work is so undesirable that it's considered punishment for others.

It also bears noting that the enforcement of laws should not be done by the same people who are creating the laws. In other words, members of the leadership committee should refrain from being actively involved in the corporal punishment, if that's the route your community decides to take. As we discussed earlier, the security element within the community serves two functions: defending from threats outside the community, as well as enforcing the laws within. If the community has sufficient population, the ideal would be for these two functions to be performed by separate groups. An analogy would be having a sheriff's department for handling law enforcement and a National Guard for handling outside threats. With that said, in our current society, the law enforcement agencies do not truly get involved with the punishment phase. While many county jails are overseen by the sheriff's department, the deputies making arrests are not the same individuals deciding on appropriate penalties. This division of duties is important to preserve the impartiality of those creating and those enforcing the laws.

When it comes to enacting new laws, great care should be taken in how they are written as well as communicated. Personally, I've always felt that if an average third-grade student cannot understand the law as it is written, it should be reevaluated. While asking an experienced attorney to assist with crafting a new law would be a great idea, he or she should be instructed to use plain English and avoid what we might call "legalese." As for communicating new laws, if possible they

PERSONALITY CONFLICTS

Personality conflicts, more than anything else, will make or break your group. If people can't find a way to get along with one another, no amount of food or equipment on the planet will be enough to keep the group intact. The clan doesn't need to be ridiculously tight-knit like some sort of idealized commune. That's just not realistic. But the group members need to respect one another, and they need to be able to work through the inevitable problems that crop up.

Just one bad apple can ruin the whole bunch. All it takes is one person sowing dissent in the ranks, so to speak, and it can all come crashing down. A good leader will watch for signs of trouble and do everything they can to curtail the problem before it gets worse.

should be posted in one or more areas that are easily accessible to the community members, as well as discussed in town meetings.

REFUGEES

One of the first acts of law that will need to be created will be rules pertaining to those who show up at the perimeter of the community and request access. After all, each person allowed in will be one more mouth that needs to be fed. I suggest following these guidelines:

1. If the person is known to own, or can prove ownership of, property within the community, that individual has a right to be allowed in. Such proof could be in the form of identification showing the address or perhaps another resident vouching for them.

2. If the person is a family member of a current resident, and said resident acknowledges responsibility for him or her, that individual is allowed in.

3. If the person is able to prove he or she possesses specific skills that are desirable within the community, such as medical expertise, that individual is allowed in. This will require some form of vetting process, of course, likely involving any current residents possessing similar skills. For example, a local doctor could interview a potential new community member who purports to be a trained EMT.

Absent any property or familial connection to the community or the ability to offer necessary skills and experience, refugees should be sent on their way. If supplies are sufficient to allow some charity, perhaps they might be given a small care package of food and water. If not, so be it. I know it sounds harsh and cruel, but the needs of the community members come first.

You have essentially two options for removing refugees from the immediate area. The first is to just deny them access, at gunpoint if necessary (and, yes, it will very likely come to that). You don't detain them but explain in no uncertain terms they need to move along. The other option is to escort them along a specific route through the town to the other side. Each approach has its pros and cons.

If you outright deny refugees access and ask them to be on their way, you run the risk of them attempting to enter the community through an unobservable point, say, through a forest that borders the community. While that area should be patrolled, you likely won't have the resources to keep it under 24/7 surveillance. The good point about this approach is that if it works the way it should, those from outside won't see what's inside at all.

On the other hand, by escorting refugees through the community, you are better able to keep an eye on them and ensure they've moved on. But, by default, they'll get something of a guided tour of the community. This puts them in a position to either use that knowledge against you or trade that information to someone else down the line.

With either solution, it is important that all involved understand that the rules need to be enforced equally and to the letter. While on rare occasion some unique circumstance may crop up that may warrant a bending of the rules, decisions cannot be made on a whim just because the refugee is attractive, charming, or possesses some other superficial quality. The guards at each entry point should be given an ongoing list of desirable skills. If a refugee purports to possess any of those skills, there should be a location near the gate where he or she can be detained until questioned further.

While the needs of communities will vary a bit based upon their exact population, skills that will likely be the most desirable include

- medical (including natural and herbal remedies)
- dental
- veterinary
- blacksmithing
- security

- gunsmithing and reloading
- food preservation

Office drones, trophy wives, and middle-management types need not apply.

QUARANTINING POTENTIAL NEW MEMBERS

All those who are granted access to the community as potential new members should be placed into quarantine for at least a couple days. They should be examined thoroughly by available medical staff to ensure they are not carrying diseases or parasites. If they are, and the conditions are treatable, by all means do what can be done for them. What you want to prevent is the introduction of new problems on top of existing ones.

The quarantine should be located near the outskirts of the community if possible. This will help prevent the spread of any diseases the newcomers may be carrying. If nothing else, consider setting up a few tents in a vacant lot. Interaction with those under quarantine should be limited to medical and security personnel.

During this quarantine time, the individuals should also be questioned about the world at large, or at least the parts of the world they traveled through to get to the community. What did they witness themselves? What rumors might they have heard? How reliable do they feel that information truly is? This information-gathering process could be crucial to the survival of the community.

This is also the time when you can educate the individuals on the basic rules of the community. There's no need to go into intimate details; they'll learn by doing soon enough. But, should the community have any specific rules that differ greatly from what might be considered basic common sense, inform these new members to prevent them from inadvertently getting into trouble.

¤ ¤ ¤ ¤

There is safety in numbers, particularly when it comes to long-term scenarios. While you might feel those who currently live around you are far from being preppers, the fact is that those who survive the initial disaster will all be survivalists, whether they wanted to be or not. By making plans ahead of time, you can be in a great position to be a valuable asset to the community.

CHAPTER 12

FINDERS KEEPERS: SCAVENGING THE WASTELAND

We've started sending out small groups, just three or four people at a time, to scrounge around the immediate area and bring back whatever supplies they can find. They've been fortunate so far in that they've not run into too many other parties doing the same thing. There have been a few sightings here and there, but no skirmishes or violence at all.

The scavenging groups are all pretty young, for the most part. Teenagers, mostly, with a couple of adults in the mix. They're quick, strong, and know the area very well.

They've not found much in the way of canned goods or bottled water, as most of that had been scrounged up pretty quickly. But, they've been locating a good supply of batteries, a pretty eclectic assortment of medications, and even some much-needed pet food.

The groups are based out of the high school. They put the word out that if there is anything specific you need, such as eyeglasses or a certain kind of medication, to let them know and they'll add it to a list they're maintaining on a dry erase board. No promises, of course, but they'll keep their eyes open.

While they've not had any violent encounters so far, the endeavor hasn't been without risk or injury. Jenny and Dan's oldest daughter, Hannah,, sprained her ankle pretty good while being chased by a few dogs. Luckily, she found an unlocked car and was able to get inside, then call for help. They each have little handheld radios they can use to keep in touch with each other, which is one reason batteries are high on the scavenge list.

I fear, though, that one of these trips will result in an altercation with predators even more dangerous, ones that walk on two legs instead of four.

In the last chapter, I mentioned the idea of doing asset assessments, in which you would take stock of what's available in your area in terms of food, water, and other resources. The focus was on obvious things, such as locking down any area pharmacies to hopefully prevent looters and collecting canned food from school cafeteria kitchens.

Here, let's look at some supply sources that might not be quite as obvious. None of them are sure things, of course. Could be someone beat you to it or perhaps the supplies weren't there at the outset of the disaster. But each of these sources is worthy of consideration.

WATER

By now, you should know that the water heater in your home can be a source for emergency water. Think bigger, though. Just about every building that is equipped with a bathroom will have a water heater somewhere. Gas stations, convenience stores, libraries, office buildings— you name it and it probably has water stored inside. That little boutique craft store on the corner might not have much in the way of survival equipment but it probably has 30 or more gallons of clean water sitting there, ready to be drained and taken away. And since it isn't an obvious source for food or supplies, that water is probably still there.

While you're at it, check for water at any exterior spigots on the building. If it is lacking a handle, you'll need a sillcock key. These handy tools can be found at many hardware stores. It looks something like a miniature version of the classic four-way tire iron. Use the key just as you would a handle on the spigot.

All water drained from these sources should be filtered or purified, just in case. While the water may have been clean when it entered the building, take no chances. A waterborne illness isn't anything to mess around with.

Check the fire department for tender vehicles. These are the trucks that carry and deliver water to fire scenes. You might find upwards of 1,000 gallons of water on hand. They are also capable of taking water in from various sources such as ponds, lakes, and even swimming pools and delivering the water through pressurized hoses. If the trucks are operational, they could be used for transporting water to areas of the community in dire need. This option in particular should be seen as a very last resort, as draining water from these sources may endanger lives that could be saved through the proper use of firefighting equipment.

FOOD AND DRY GOODS

Searching stores and homes is for amateurs. The big stockpiles are found in warehouses and distribution centers. Of course, you might not be the first person to realize this, and there could well be folks already occupying the warehouse when you get there. Use extreme caution when approaching these sources, just in case.

Most retail stores lack any sort of extensive storage space. It might still be worthwhile to search the stockrooms in case anything was missed. Some retailers have multiple stockrooms. Check behind every "Employees Only" door you find. Tread carefully in areas that were used as cold storage; if the power has been out for a while, the stench might be overpowering.

Keep an eye out for any semi-trailers stuck on the road or parked in lots. Each and every one of them should be searched. Again, though, be wary of refrigerated trailers. These will typically have a cooling unit installed on the front of the trailer, facing the truck. Any food in these refrigerated trailers, called "reefers" by many truck drivers, will probably have gone bad.

We often don't think much about it unless we get stopped at a railroad crossing, but quite a bit of retail goods are still transported by rail in the

United States. Check any local railyards as well as every inch of track in the area for stopped trains. Go through them car by car.

Don't overlook delivery service vehicles such as those used by the UPS, FedEx, and even the post office. You probably won't find a whole lot of food that was headed for delivery the day everything crashed, but you might find other useful items. Bear in mind that tampering with the mail is a rather severe offense, and I would only suggest doing so in the direst of circumstances. Who knows? You might intercept a shipment of gear and supplies headed to your local survival author's home.

SELF-STORAGE FACILITIES

It is sometimes easier to justify scavenging supplies from a business location rather than a home or even one of these storage units. A business, especially a chain location that is part of a large corporation,

SELF-STORAGE CACHES

Caching refers to storing supplies away from home, typically along some sort of planned route, that will give you the ability to resupply as you travel. While most self-storage facilities are located in urban areas and thus in places you want to avoid in the aftermath of a major disaster, many are found out in the sticks. For example, I know of at least four such businesses within a 20-mile radius of my home that are each pretty much in the middle of nowhere.

Even the smallest units could work well as cache locations. They are usually climate controlled, so you don't need to worry about supplies getting too warm in the summer or freezing solid in the winter, at least as long as utility services are still running. The places located out in the sticks aren't likely to be looted right away.

If the budget allows, you could consider renting a unit large enough for you to bed down in for a night or three as you and your group plan your next move. If you split the cost among the members of your group, the individual financial hit will obviously be less.

is seen as being owned by a faceless entity. A home or storage unit is filled with stuff we see as having been owned by an individual or family.

The vast majority of these units are filled with household goods and clothing. Boxes of Christmas decorations, old furniture, quasi-antiques that someone is convinced will be worth money someday. However, diligent searching may uncover tools, building supplies, camping gear, hunting equipment, and other useful items.

VEHICLES

Cars, trucks, and vans are rife with potential. Start with a detailed search of the interior, including the glove box and under the seats. Don't forget to check above the visors, inside the armrest, and the door pockets.

Pop the trunk and see what treasures might be hidden there. If the keys are missing and the trunk unlock button isn't working, check the rear seats. Many newer vehicles are equipped with rear seats that fold down, allowing you to access the trunk. If you're able to squeeze your way into there, look for a release latch or lever inside the trunk that will pop open the lid.

Assuming the car hasn't been scavenged yet, you could find a plethora of goodies, from water bottles to spare clothes. This is especially true if there was an evacuation effort and there are vehicles that ended up stranded and then abandoned.

As for the vehicles themselves, many will still have fuel. This can be drained, or you could use the vehicle as the fuel container and leave it until needed. Most auto parts stores as well as repair garages have fuel siphons you can use to remove the fuel. Punching a hole in the gas tank to drain the fuel is actually quite difficult, despite what you may have read online. There's no space under the vehicle to generate any power in a hammer swing to pound a screwdriver through the bottom of the tank. Plus, the tank isn't exactly delicate in construction.

Depending on your needs, there's a lot you can do with an abandoned car. The seat belts can be removed and used as cordage. If you have some basic tools available to you, the hood can be removed and used as part of a shelter or as a sled to pull your gear along in the snow. If you're building a shelter, use the upholstery and padding from the car seats for insulation.

Left intact, the car can be used as a large dehydrator. Put your jerky, cut fruit and veggies, or other such vittles on cookie sheets and place them on the dash and seats of the car. Roll up the windows, leaving an inch or so open for air flow. You might want to cover the food with lightweight cloth to prevent bugs from landing on it. Check the food from time to time until it is ready.

MEDICAL FACILITIES

Any medical facility will be a fast target for looters. The list of such locations includes:

- hospitals
- urgent care facilities
- walk-in clinics
- assisted care facilities
- pharmacies
- dentists

Once the rule of law has disappeared, the addicts and their suppliers will be out in droves looking to score. The good news is that most of them won't be scooping up the antibiotics and other healing drugs. They'll be looking for the narcotics. Of course, they likely won't leave the area neat and tidy once they're done searching.

When searching for useful supplies, you'll need to look in every little nook and cranny you can find. Hospitals, clinics, and the like tend to make use of every available inch of storage space. Next time you visit a medical care facility, poke around in the cupboards and drawers when the nurse leaves the room. Don't take anything; this isn't an invitation to steal. Just make a note of all the different things that are stored in just one exam room.

Most hospitals and some clinics are equipped with emergency generators, which could prove useful to a post-apocalyptic survivor. However, the generators are invariably very large and thus not easily removed and transported elsewhere. Poke around a bit and you might find fuel that was designated for the generators but went unused.

If there's a cafeteria onsite, there may be some food or water left to scavenge. Same goes for all assisted care facilities.

A word of caution, though. As I mentioned, medical facilities are going to be primary targets for looters very early on. Some of them may decide to set up shop, so to speak, and actually occupy the building. Approach and enter these buildings with both eyes wide open and be wary of any signs that people are hanging around.

You may also need to contend will the issue of the deceased. To be blunt, there are likely going to be a large number of bodies in places like hospitals and nursing homes. These will need to be disposed of, hopefully in a respectful manner. Be prepared, though, with masks and gloves when entering these facilities. Some find that a smear of vapor rub on the upper lip can help mask the stench.

JANITORIAL SUPPLIES

When searching any business, from hospitals to factories, see if you can find the janitorial supply closet. There, you'll not only find all manner of cleaning equipment but probably large stashes of toilet paper, soap, paper towels, and other useful items. Check in every restroom in the building, too. While the quality may be on the industrial side rather than comfortable, it will still be better than keeping a stack of old newspapers in the bathroom.

FACTORIES

While you may not be fortunate enough to live near a factory that assembled top-notch survival equipment, odds are there are at least a couple of manufacturing facilities in your community. There are all sorts of useful things found in factories, no matter what they make.

Wooden pallets can be taken apart and used for building material or just as firewood. I hesitate to suggest they be burned indoors or used to cook food simply because you may not know whether any chemicals soaked into the wood.

Most factories will be filled with tools, both powered and hand operated. In fact, outside of hardware stores and auto repair garages, factories may turn out to be the best source for the tools necessary during the rebuilding process. Depending on what they manufactured, there may be lumber, sheet metal, and other materials that will prove useful, not to mention fasteners like screws, nuts, bolts, and all sorts of other hardware.

At a minimum, there should be one or two first aid kits on site. Larger operations might even have a room devoted to medical supplies, though more and more factories are doing away with such things in favor of using every inch of floor space for manufacturing and profit.

Check in the breakroom, if there is one, and see if the vending machines have escaped being pillaged. While you're there, you might as well check in the employee lockers as well as the office area.

MOTELS

Scavenging in motels will be sort of like busting open a piñata. There's no way to know what you'll find until you get in there. Could be most or even all of the rooms were unoccupied at the time disaster hit and, thus, all that is there is what you'd typically find in a motel room: sheets, blankets, and pillows of dubious cleanliness, miniature toiletries, and a couple of single-serve packets of coffee.

Granted, those coffee packets might be worth their weight in gold after a collapse. Snatch them up, along with any you find behind the front counter and in storage closets. Toiletries may have barter value as well.

Obviously, any luggage found in the rooms should be checked for anything useful. You'll probably find nothing more exciting than vacation outfits but there could be flashlights, batteries, snacks, bottles of water, and perhaps even a pocketknife or two.

A post-collapse community that lacks a proper hospital might be able to use local motels as impromptu medical facilities. They have lots of beds and would make it somewhat easy to keep sick patients quarantined if necessary.

SPECIALTY SHOPS

Big-box retailers are likely to be the primary targets for many scavengers, but there are any number of strip malls and other smaller shopping centers that have stores worth exploring for a few necessities.

Batteries in all common sizes can be found in toy stores, usually near the cash register.

Hobby stores will also have batteries, along with various types of cordage, from twine to rope and more.

Check pet stores for various sizes of bandages and other medical items, including antiseptics and other types of medication.

RECONNAISSANCE

Don't go into any building blind. Meaning, always take a bit of time to check things out first. Look for indications that the building is occupied, such as footprints coming and going or other signs of disturbance. The last thing you want is to surprise someone in their new home. Think about how you'd react in their position.

Always plan an exit strategy, too. Know how you'll get out of the room and the building. Avoid going into an area that only has one exit. That said, think outside the box a bit and understand that virtually any window can be a door in a pinch, provided you're able to either open it or smash it.

SCAVENGING EQUIPMENT

Heading out into the world to find more food and other supplies isn't a task to be taken lightly. This isn't a quick run to the grocery store to pick up a dozen eggs and a loaf of bread. These sorts of outings may require some specialized gear.

ENTRY TOOLS

While it would be great if all doors and windows were unlocked, or even better if you had the only keys in town for everything, the reality

LOCKPICKING

Being able to finesse your way through a locked door is a great skill to possess. The basics of picking locks isn't difficult to learn. Hell, two of my sons taught themselves how to do it over the course of a week or so. In many states, you can legally own lockpick tools, but you need to be careful about carrying them around as they can be considered burglary tools.

One of the best resources for learning this skill is the Lockpicking Lawyer channel on YouTube. An excellent source for the tools themselves is Sparrows Lock Picks (SparrowsLockPicks.com).

is that you'll probably have to force your way in. There are tools that will make this job easier.

Pry bars are probably the first line of defense against locked entry points. A flat bar will provide the leverage needed for many doors and most windows, while a smaller one, such as a large screwdriver, can help in tight quarters.

Bolt cutters are also good to have, in case you need to get through a fence or cut through a chain. Depending on the size of the latter, cutting through the shackle on the lock might prove easier.

If you have a way to handle the weight easily, a car jack can also be handy for opening rolling overhead doors and gates. You might even forgo bringing one and just scavenge one from an abandoned vehicle near your target building.

SEARCH AND RECOVERY TOOLS

You'll probably need a flashlight, as many buildings are very dark inside without power. However, in an effort to keep your efforts at least somewhat discreet, keep the light on the lowest setting possible. Or, cover the lens with duct tape except for a tiny pinhole opening. That will still provide enough light to see what you're doing. A headlamp will allow you to keep your hands free and the same application of tape will work just fine with it.

Depending on the overall situation, the time elapsed since disaster struck, and a variety of other factors, there's a good chance that you'll be dealing with broken glass and other debris. Protect yourself by wearing thick-soled boots and work gloves. Avoid bright clothing and stick with neutral, subdued colors to blend in with your surroundings.

You'll need a way to bring your scavenged treasures back home, of course. You can only carry so much, even with a good-sized backpack. There are several options, including lawn carts, wheelbarrows, and even shopping carts. Ideally you won't be embarking on these jaunts by yourself, as just about every realistic or practical conveyance will require one or both hands. Having someone else with you provides not just another set of eyes, but an unencumbered person who is in a better position to react to threats.

If you and your partner must separate, stay in communication with one another. Two-way radios are ideal for this, particularly because you likely won't be out of range from each other. An earpiece will reduce the risk of someone else overhearing the entire conversation.

RETURNING HOME

If at all possible, take different routes to and from your targets with each trip. This will hopefully reduce the odds of someone focusing on your own home or community for their own scavenging endeavors. Watch your back and pay close attention to your surroundings. If things seem to be going awry, ditch your goodies and get out of the area as quickly as possible. Better to do that than risk injury, or worse, in an altercation.

APPENDIX

Today marks one year exactly since the lights went out. We've endured harsh weather, a truly obscene body count, and more trials and tribulations than I care to revisit here. Yet, for all that, I think maybe, just maybe, we've come out ahead.

We had a celebration of sorts in the park up the road. The community leaders (Sean, Amy, Jed, and Chris) each gave a short speech, patting us all on the back for coming as far as we have. Father Mulcahy led us in a prayer, remembering those we've lost. Those who gave their lives in battle were specially recognized. While most of us didn't have much to spare, we each brought something to contribute to the festivities. Stacy and her husband brought a couple plates of fried rabbit with a honey butter dipping sauce. They've always had bunnies, and have been doing a brisk trade at their place. Ian brought some roasted venison from a deer he'd bagged yesterday. Between those two contributions, everyone was able to get at least a little fresh meat, which is something of a treat these days. For our part, we brought a good-sized pile of fingerling potatoes we'd peeled and grilled. Maybe not the same as french fries, but still mighty tasty with a little salt.

Our little community has settled into a routine that is almost comfortable. I mean, yeah, we have to keep our eyes open for threats, and our security patrols are still fraught with anxiety about what they'll find around the next corner. But just the fact that there IS a routine to our lives makes us feel better about the future. Long gone are the days when we'd wake up and wonder where the next meal would be coming from. We might not have much in the way of food, certainly nothing like we did back when trucks were running and stores were well stocked. But we don't go to bed hungry.

I think one of the biggest changes in the last year has been how close we now are to one another. We actually talk to our neighbors, those next door and down the road. We aren't afraid to ask for a lending hand to mend a fence, knowing that tomorrow we'll repay the favor by helping them with bringing down a dying tree.

Our kids have adapted well to a life without Facebook and video chats. Children are indeed resilient.

Perhaps the thing I noticed the most at the celebration was something that had been missing for a long time but has finally come back to our little corner of the world—

Hope.

It has been said that preppers and survivalists are "doom and gloom" types, always talking about pandemics, nuclear war, and natural disasters. In my experience, that is actually far from the case. While we may worry about end-of-the-world scenarios more than the average person, we are taking steps to make things better in the wake of disasters, rather than just throwing our hands in the air and accepting the worst as unavoidable. If nothing else, preppers are actually rather optimistic, when you get right down to it. We recognize that bad things happen in the world but believe that by preparing for them ahead of time, we can beat the odds and come out ahead in the end.

Personally, I truly hope we never do experience disasters of the magnitude we've been discussing. I rather like having reliable access to Netflix, flush toilets, and the occasional handful of Doritos. At the same time, though, it is just common sense to be prepared for whatever life might decide to throw our way.

As you go through your own long-term survival planning, you might notice a change in your thinking, and this change might alarm you. It is not at all uncommon for someone who's been prepping for years and years to start to actually long for a disaster to hit. Not in a tragic sense—not wanting to see mass death and destruction. But, rather, you desire sort of a real-life test. You want to see that all your prepping wasn't for naught.

This is normal. You're not weird. Well, maybe you are weird, but this isn't a symptom of being so.

Thinking about a world without law, without rules, gives many people a tingle. The idea of being able to just take what you need from a store, without worrying about payment, is exciting. I mean, one of the most common tropes in post-apocalyptic fiction is when the hero, down to his last can of ravioli and three bullets, comes across a store that has miraculously avoided being looted down to bare shelves. He finds everything from handguns and ammo to a brand-new leather duster and sets out on the trail again.

On top of that is the very human desire to be able to truthfully say, "I told you so!" A major disaster, and our successfully overcoming it, would be validation for all our efforts and planning. No longer would we feel it necessary to defend our beliefs or argue with a spouse about expenditures. We can just let loose with a righteous, "Ha! I was right!"

Sometimes students in martial arts training, having learned a few basic defensive moves, will wish for a real-world test. It isn't that they want to hurt anyone, but, rather, they want to know for certain that what they've learned will work out on the street. I mean, it's one thing to break a choke hold in the dojo or gymnasium, where if you screw it up, the instructor will simply admonish you to try it again; it's quite another to have some Hell's Angel wannabe breathing beer-breath down your neck as his heavily tattooed forearm draws ever tighter around your throat.

As that vague yet ubiquitous group of people we call "they" often admonish, be careful what you wish for.

A disaster of the degree that we've been discussing, one that would almost certainly result in a total societal collapse, won't be fun and games. Not unless one of your favorite games involves choosing a burial plot in your own backyard.

Let's take a little closer look at just one end-of-the-world scenario. Way back in chapter 1, we talked about EMP. While we know, at least in a practical sense, what the basic ramifications would be—a breakdown of the electrical grid—we honestly can't say for sure exactly how bad things could get. For example, an EMP of sufficient magnitude could cause affected planes to crash. Given that there are, on average, about five thousand planes in the air over the continental United States at any given time, that's an awful lot of possible debris, as well as a fair number of bodies, coming down at high velocity.

Then you have the thousands of people who are occupying hospital beds at any given time, many of whom are relying upon some form of life support. While most hospitals have generator backups to be used during power failures, an EMP may cause them to be inoperable as well. It's safe to say hospitals and long-term care facilities won't be pleasant places to be after such an event.

EMP-induced vehicle crashes would undoubtedly injure or kill thousands more. Just because the engines stop running doesn't mean the cars and trucks come to a halt. Many drivers, who only seconds before had been cruising along at seventy miles per hour on an interstate highway, and now facing the sudden loss of power steering and power brakes, will panic and lose control of their vehicles.

In a nation where being overweight, even obese, is considered the norm rather than the exception, countless more people will drop dead from heart attacks and related issues in the days immediately following the EMP. When suddenly faced with having to walk miles to get home from where the car died, many won't make it.

In short, there will be an awful lot of dead bodies littering the landscape. And that's just within hours of the initial event. Doesn't sound like a whole lot of fun to me; how about you?

Another thing to bear in mind is that disasters are rarely ever single-natured. By that, I mean it isn't often that the misery stops with the initial event. Instead, it often works like dominoes. For example, let's stick with the EMP scenario a bit longer. Wildfires hit the West Coast of the United States with frightening regularity. Currently, we are able to combat them using the best firefighting technology around. However, what if those firefighters weren't there, which seems likely in a post-EMP situation? What if buckets of lake water tossed by hand were the epitome of our available firefighting abilities?

If disasters are only going to beget or compound other crises, then what's the point of prepping? Why in the world would someone want to live through all that death and destruction?

Because surviving beats the alternative. Beats it by a long shot.

Most preppers and survivalists are familiar with the acronym TEOTWAWKI. For the uninitiated, this stands for The End Of The World As We Know It. It refers to the sorts of disasters we've been discussing, events that go far beyond a simple three-day blizzard.

Here's the thing about that phrase: Most people concentrate on the first part of it—The End Of The World. The latter half is often seen merely as an intensifier, a qualifier, if you will. Really, what it is saying is the event will bring about an end to the world *as we know it to be today*. It isn't saying the world is going to be utterly destroyed, but that it is going to change and be completely different from what we've known before.

History has shown that civilizations rarely disappear completely or instantly from the face of the earth. Instead, the collapsed society and culture typically are absorbed by those in the area. When the Roman Empire fell, it wasn't as if every single Roman just up and died, leaving behind nothing but burned-out ruins. In fact, it was a series of events over the course of a few hundred years that led to the eventual decline and fall of the empire. Hell, some historians suggest the Roman Empire never did actually "fall" but instead went through several transformations and eventually morphed into what we now call the medieval world.

The point of that short history lesson is that should our current society collapse for whatever reason, it won't simply just cease to exist. It will change, people will adapt, and a new society will arise from the ashes of the old. As kids today like to say, that's just how we roll.

Human beings are nothing if not adaptable. In only the last hundred years or so, we've seen countless wars, including nuclear weapons dropped on Japan. The Spanish flu pandemic killed off tens of millions of people around the world. We've experienced natural disasters, from earthquakes to tsunamis, hurricanes to drought. Stock markets have crashed and various currencies become worthless.

Any one of those events could have been enough to send humanity into a tailspin, were it not for the tenacity of humankind.

Should an EMP take down the grid, should the Yellowstone Caldera finally blow, I have little doubt that a significant percentage of the population will survive. They will then become the forebears of a new world, a new society, maybe not created from whole cloth but certainly unlike what we've seen before.

By planning ahead, you can be there to see what comes next. I told you, we preppers and survivalists are optimists!

CHECKLISTS

As you progress through your long-term preparedness planning, use these checklists to help keep you on track. You'll no doubt notice that there is an awful lot of stuff listed here. Consider these lists as the ideal for which to strive, understanding that compiling every single item may not be feasible.

WATER

- ❏ water filtration system
- ❏ spare filters
- ❏ nylon scrubbing pad for cleaning ceramic filters
- ❏ kettle for boiling water
- ❏ coffee filters
- ❏ water purification tablets
- ❏ non-scented chlorine bleach
- ❏ pool shock
- ❏ 5- or 7-gallon containers
- ❏ quart or liter water bottles

FOOD PRESERVATION AND STORAGE

- ❏ pressure canner
- ❏ canning jars, lids, and rings
- ❏ 5-gallon buckets (from delis, bakeries, etc.)
- ❏ Gamma lids for buckets
- ❏ dehydrator
- ❏ window screening (for solar dehydration)
- ❏ zip-top bags (quart and gallon sizes)
- ❏ coolers/ice chests

FOOD PREPARATION

- ❏ grill (propane or charcoal)
- ❏ propane tanks (if applicable)
- ❏ charcoal
- ❏ firewood
- ❏ camp stove
- ❏ rocket stove
- ❏ cast-iron skillet
- ❏ cast-iron Dutch oven
- ❏ utensils
- ❏ paper plates, bowls, cups
- ❏ stainless steel mixing bowls
- ❏ meat thermometer
- ❏ aluminum foil (heavy-duty)
- ❏ manual can openers
- ❏ tripod for suspending pots above open fire
- ❏ mess kits

MEDICAL SUPPLIES

- ❏ pain relievers
- ❏ ibuprofen
- ❏ acetaminophen
- ❏ naproxen
- ❏ aspirin
- ❏ stomach medicines
- ❏ Pepto-Bismol
- ❏ Imodium
- ❏ antacids
- ❏ cough/cold medicines
- ❏ cough drops
- ❏ vitamin C tablets or lozenges
- ❏ prescription medications
- ❏ adhesive bandages
- ❏ gauze pads (various sizes)
- ❏ elastic wraps (for strains/sprains)
- ❏ pressure bandages
- ❏ surgical tape
- ❏ rubbing alcohol
- ❏ hydrogen peroxide
- ❏ tweezers
- ❏ magnifying glass
- ❏ first aid manual
- ❏ natural remedies textbook
- ❏ eye bandages
- ❏ CPR mask
- ❏ cotton balls
- ❏ surgical kit (if trained in proper usage)
- ❏ scissors
- ❏ nitrile gloves
- ❏ surgical masks
- ❏ thermometer
- ❏ stethoscope
- ❏ blood pressure cuff
- ❏ dental injury kit
- ❏ clove oil

HYGIENE

- toilet paper
- baby wipes
- hand sanitizer
- hand soap
- shampoo
- wash cloths
- bath towels
- camp shower
- toothbrushes
- toothpaste
- dental floss
- deodorant
- moisturizing lotion
- lip balm
- sunscreen
- insect repellent

SECURITY AND DEFENSE

For each mature member of your family or group:

- handgun with 1,000 rounds ammunition
- handgun holster
- rifle or shotgun with 1,000 rounds ammunition
- rifle sling
- combat knife
- firearm cleaning kit with appropriate supplies for each firearm
- ballistic vest
- binoculars
- 2 to 3 air rifles with several boxes of ammunition (useful for teaching accuracy and proper rifle care, as well as hunting small game)
- two-way radios
- glass bottles for Molotov cocktails
- wireless driveway alarms
- trip wire
- bug-out bags for use during patrols

TOOLS

- hammers
- hand saws
- wrenches (box and open end, SAE and metric)
- pliers
- screwdrivers (various sizes, Phillips and slotted)
- duct tape
- paracord
- come-along
- pry bar
- axe
- splitting wedge
- loppers
- shovel
- hoe
- garden cart or wheelbarrow
- hand trowels

- string
- tape measure
- plastic sheeting or tarps
- grommet repair kit
- bungee cords
- pocket knives and/or multitools
- work gloves
- safety glasses
- chainsaw with extra chains
- fuel for chainsaw
- chain sharpening kit
- files and sharpening stones for blades
- zip ties
- wire cutters
- bolt cutters
- WD-40

LIGHTING AND POWER

- generator (solar or gas powered)
- fuel
- extension cords
- candles
- candle wicks
- oil lamps
- lamp oil
- lamp wicks

- batteries
- solar-powered battery charger
- chemical light sticks (i.e., snap lights)
- LED flashlights
- LED headlamps
- strike anywhere matches

BARTER OR TRADE GOODS

- ❏ tobacco
- ❏ alcoholic beverages
- ❏ matches
- ❏ heirloom seeds
- ❏ candy/chocolate
- ❏ instant coffee
- ❏ tea bags
- ❏ salt
- ❏ needles and thread
- ❏ honey
- ❏ sugar
- ❏ butane lighters
- ❏ strike anywhere matches
- ❏ toiletries (soap, shampoo, toothpaste)
- ❏ baking soda
- ❏ vinegar
- ❏ condoms

BUG-OUT BAG

- ❏ backpack
- ❏ food for 2 to 3 days
- ❏ water bottles (2)
- ❏ water purification tablets or portable filtration system
- ❏ maps of area
- ❏ spare ammunition for weapons
- ❏ binoculars
- ❏ first aid kit
- ❏ two-way radio with spare batteries
- ❏ emergency blanket
- ❏ fire starting supplies
- ❏ LED flashlight with spare batteries
- ❏ knife or multitool
- ❏ paracord or other cordage
- ❏ compass
- ❏ small notebook and pencil

MISCELLANEOUS

- ❏ mouse or rat traps (for vermin as well as food procurement)
- ❏ maps of surrounding area
- ❏ ham radio
- ❏ CB radio
- ❏ board games
- ❏ decks of playing cards
- ❏ dice
- ❏ flea and tick repellents (for pets)
- ❏ fire extinguishers
- ❏ pencils, pens
- ❏ blank paper or notebooks
- ❏ sewing supplies (needles, thread, patches, etc.)
- ❏ safety pins
- ❏ clothes pins
- ❏ spare blankets and bed linens
- ❏ heirloom seeds

RECOMMENDED BOOKS

It would be nigh impossible to compile one single book containing all of the information you will likely need to survive, and even better *thrive*, during a societal collapse. Therefore, I've always advocated assembling a small library, consisting of several volumes that each serve a specific purpose. I recommend acquiring these books in hard copy format, so you won't be dependent upon electricity to access the knowledge inside them.

FOOD PRESERVATION AND STORAGE

Canning and Preserving for Dummies, 2nd edition
by Amelia Jeanroy and Karen Ward (Hoboken, NJ: Wiley Publishing, 2009)

Root Cellaring: Natural Cold Storage of Fruits and Vegetables, 2nd edition
by Mike and Nancy Bubel (North Adams, MA: Storey Publishing, 1991)

Ball Complete Book of Home Preserving: 400 Delicious and Creative Recipes for Today
by Judi Kingery and Lauren Devine (Toronto, Canada: Robert Rose, 2006)

HOMESTEADING
The Encyclopedia of Country Living: The Original Manual for Living Off the Land and Doing It Yourself, 50th anniversary edition
by Carla Emery(Seattle, WA: Sasquatch Books,, 2019)

Storey's Basic Country Skills: A Practical Guide to Self-Reliance
by John and Martha Storey (North Adams, MA: Storey Publishing, 2010)

The Mini-Farming Bible: The Complete Guide to Self-Sufficiency on ¼ Acre
by Brett L. Markham (New York: Skyhorse, 2014)

Creating the Low-Budget Homestead
By Steven D. Gregersen (Independently published, 2018)

Storey's Curious Compendium of Practical and Obscure Skills: 214 Things You Can Actually Learn How to Do
by How-To Experts at Storey Publishing (North Adams, MA: Storey Publishing, LLC, 2020)

MEDICAL AND FIRST AID
Prepper's Natural Medicine: Lifesaving Herbs, Essential Oils, and Natural Remedies for When There Is No Doctor
by Cat Ellis (Berkeley, CA: Ulysses Press, 2015)

A Field Guide to Medicinal Plants and Herbs: Eastern and Central North America (Peterson Field Guides), 3rd edition
by Steven Foster and James A. Duke (Boston, MA: Mariner Books, 2014)

Peterson Field Guide to Western Medicinal Plants and Herbs
by Steven Foster and Christopher Hobbs (New York: HarperCollins Harcourt, 2002)

Medicinal Plants of the Southern Appalachians, 4th edition
by Patricia Kyritsi Howell (Mountain City, GA: BotanoLogos, 2006)

PDR for Herbal Medicines
by Thomson Healthcare (Montvale, NJ: Thomson Healthcare, Inc., 2007)

The Survival Medicine Handbook: A Guide for When Help Is Not on the Way, 4th edition
by Joseph and Amy Alton (Weston, FL: Doom and Bloom, 2021)

Alton's Antibiotics and Infectious Disease: The Layman's Guide to Available Antibacterials in Austere Settings
by Joseph and Amy Alton (Weston, FL: Alton First Aid, LLC, 2018)

Where There Is No Doctor: A Village Health Care Handbook, revised edition
by David Werner, Carol Thuman, and Jane Maxwell (Berkeley, CA: Hesperian Health Guides, 2022)

Where There Is No Dentist
by Murray Dickson (Berkeley, CA: Hesperian Health Guides, 2021)

US Army Special Forces Medical Handbook
by Glen C. Craig (Boulder, CO: Paladin Press, 1988)

SECURITY AND DEFENSE
Prepper's Home Defense: Security Strategies to Protect Your Family by Any Means Necessary
by Jim Cobb (Berkeley, CA: Ulysses Press, 2012)

Holding Your Ground: Preparing for Defense If It All Falls Apart
by Joe Nobody (Augusta, ME: PrepperPress.com, 2011)

GENERAL PREPAREDNESS
The Prepper's Pocket Guide: 101 Easy Things You Can Do to Ready Your Home for a Disaster
by Bernie Carr (Berkeley, CA: Ulysses Press, 2011)

Build the Perfect Bug Out Bag: Your 72-Hour Disaster Survival Kit
by Creek Stewart (Cinncinati, OH: Betterway Books, 2012)

Build the Perfect Survival Kit, 2nd edition
by John D. McCann (Lehi, UT: Living Ready, 2013)

Emergency Food Storage and Survival Handbook: Everything You Need to Know to Keep Your Family Safe in a Crisis
by Peggy Layton (New York: Clarkson Potter, 2002)

The Prepper's Complete Book of Disaster Readiness: Life-Saving Skills, Supplies, Tactics and Plans
by Jim Cobb (Berkeley, CA: Ulysses Press, 2013)

The Unofficial Hunger Games Wilderness Survival Guide
by Creek Stewart (Lehi, UT: Living Ready Books, 2013)

Practical Self-Reliance
By John D. McCann (Poughkeepsie, NY: John D. McCann, 2014)

Be Ready for Anything: How to Survive Tornadoes, Earthquakes, Pandemics, Mass Shootings, Nuclear Disasters, and Other Life-Threatening Events
By Daisy Luther (New York: Racehorse, 2019)

WILDERNESS SKILLS

Extreme Wilderness Survival: Essential Knowledge to Survive Any Outdoor Situation Short-Term or Long-Term, with or without Gear and Alone or with Others
By Craig Caudill (Salem, MA: Page Street Publishing, 2017)

Stay Alive!: Survival Skills You Need
By John D. McCann (Iola, WI: Krause Publications, 2011)

Ultimate Wilderness Gear: Everything You Need to Know to Choose and Use the Best Outdoor Equipment
By Craig Caudill (Salem, MA: Page Street Publishing, 2018)

101 Skills You Need to Survive in the Woods: The Most Effective Wilderness Know-How on Fire-Making, Knife Work, Navigation, Shelter, Food and More
By Kevin Estela (Salem, MA: Page Street Publishing, 2019)

Surviving the Wild: Essential Bushcraft and First Aid Skills for Surviving the Great Outdoors
By Joshua Enyart (Coral Gables, FL: Mango, 2021)

MAGAZINES

There are a number of prepping or survival-related publications on the stand or available by subscription. They're great for keeping up to date with the latest information, trends, and products.

Prepper Survival Guide and *Backwoods Survival Guide*
AwesomeMagazines.com

Recoil Offgrid
Offgridweb.com

The Backwoodsman
Backwoodsmanmag.com

Backwoods Home Magazine
Backwoodshome.com

Countryside
Iamcountryside.com

Knives Illustrated
KnivesIllustrated.com

FICTION

While it might seem strange to include fictional works in a preparedness library, there is much that can be learned through reading novels and short stories. The books listed here all contain a fair amount of practical information as well as engaging and riveting stories that are very well written.

The Ashfall Trilogy

Ashfall
by Mike Mullin (Terre Haute, IN: Tanglewood Press, 2011)

Ashen Winter
by Mike Mullin (Terre Haute, IN: Tanglewood Press, 2012)

Sunrise
by Mike Mullin (Terre Haute, IN: Tanglewood Press, 2014)

The Survivalist series

The Survivalist 1 (Frontier Justice)
by Arthur T. Bradley, PhD (Scotts Valley, CA: Createspace, 2013)

The Survivalist 2 (Anarchy Rising)
by Arthur T. Bradley, PhD (Scotts Valley, CA: Createspace, 2013)

The Survivalist 3 (Judgment Day)
by Arthur T. Bradley, PhD (Scotts Valley, CA: Createspace, 2014)

The Survivalist 4 (Madness Rules)
by Arthur T. Bradley, PhD (Scotts Valley, CA: Createspace, 2014)

The Survivalist 5 (Battle Lines)
by Arthur T. Bradley, PhD (Scotts Valley, CA: Createspace, 2014)

The Survivalist 6 (Finest Hour)
by Arthur T. Bradley, PhD (Scotts Valley, CA: Createspace, 2015)

The Survivalist 7 (Last Stand)
by Arthur T. Bradley, PhD (Scotts Valley, CA: Createspace, 2015)

The Survivalist 8 (Dark Days)
by Arthur T. Bradley, PhD (Scotts Valley, CA: Createspace, 2016)

The Survivalist 9 (Freedom Lost)
by Arthur T. Bradley, PhD (Scotts Valley, CA: Createspace, 2017)

The Survivalist 10 (National Treasure)
by Arthur T. Bradley, PhD (Scotts Valley, CA: Createspace, 2017)

The Survivalist 11 (Solemn Duty)
by Arthur T. Bradley, PhD (Scotts Valley, CA: Createspace, 2018)

The Survivalist 12 (Road Home)
by Arthur T. Bradley, PhD (Scotts Valley, CA: Createspace, 2020)

The Rule of Three series

The Rule of Three
by Eric Walters (New York: Farrar, Straus and Giroux (BYR), 2014)

The Rule of Three: Fight for Power
by Eric Walters (New York: Farrar, Straus and Giroux (BYR), 2015)

The Rule of Three: Will to Survive
by Eric Walters (New York: Farrar, Straus and Giroux (BYR), 2016)

Other novels

The Fourth Dimension
by Eric Walters (New York: Penguin Teen, 2018)

The Jakarta Pandemic
by Steven Konkoly (Carmel, IN: Stribling Media, 2013)

The Pulse
by Scott B. Williams (Berkeley, CA: Ulysses Press, 2012)

If you prefer your prepper fiction heavy with action, you will want to check out the DD12 Post Apoc Army. This is a group of authors who all specialize in end of the world fiction. Find them all at DD12PostApoc.com.

INDEX

G

gardening
  choosing location, 41–42
  choosing plant, 53
  cold frames, 49–50
  companion planting, 53–55
  compost, 43–45
  container, 47
  greenhouse, 50
  heirloom seeds, 36
  hoop house, 50–52
  humanure, 45
  journal, 41
  manure, 45
  organic practices, 42
  peat moss, 47
  raised beds, 48–49
  soil amendments, 42–43
  tips, 37
  vermiculite, 46
General Mobile Radio Service
  (GMRS), 148
Goal Zero, 147

H

Hiroshima, bombing, 10
home
  as primary shelter, 115–117
  chimney sweeping, 116
  keeping cool, 117–119
  warming without fire, 117
home brewing, 168
homesteading skills, 168

horror stories, Tambora eruption, 9
hot stone cooking, 74–75
*Humanure Handbook: A Guide
  to Composting Human Manure*
  (Jenkins), 45
human waste, 105–107
  corpses, 107
hunting, 59
hygiene
  bathing, 102–103
  feminine, 104
  laundry, 100–102
  need for cleanliness, 98–99
  toilet facilities, 99–100
  tooth care, 103–104
  waste disposal, 104–107

I

Ibuprofen, 88
Ice Age, 12
insulin, 91
Irish Lumper, 7
Irish Potato Famine (1845-1852),
  7

J

Jackery, 147
journal, 41

K

knowledge
  medical, 79–80
  skills and, 92

ACKNOWLEDGMENTS

This revised and expanded edition was a long time coming. I stumbled through more than a couple of false starts along the way, leading to a fair amount of frustration for all involved.

First and foremost, I need to thank all of my readers out there. The first edition of this book has been wildly popular, and I can't express enough just how much I appreciate it. For those of you who have been patiently waiting for this new edition, I hope you enjoy it as much as I did when I finally got going on it.

To my wife, Tammy—if it weren't for your pushing and prodding me years ago, I'd still be punching a time clock somewhere. Thank you for all you do. I love you more today than yesterday, but still not as much as I will tomorrow.

To my sons, Andrew, Michael, and Thomas—you guys are all sorts of awesome. It is hard to believe how little you all were when the first edition of this book was written, and how much you've grown since then. I love you all very much.

To my amigo Chris Golden—I cannot thank you enough for all of your guidance, support, and most of all, friendship, over the years. It all means the world to me.

To my other mentor Brian Keene—I know you get sick of hearing it, but "ass in chair, fingers on keyboard" changed my life. Thank you for that, as well as all you've done to help me and guide me through the years.

To my survival and prepper crew: Craig Caudill, John McCann, Creek Stewart, Joe and Amy Alton, Pete Orndorff, and anyone else I'm forgetting—you all rock! Thank you for having my back and helping me so much over the last decade or more.

To Mike McCourt, Ryan Lee Price, Patrick Vuong, Joshua Swanagon, and Steve Barlow—you guys have all been instrumental in the development of my writing, and I can't thank you enough for that. You are all top-notch writers and editors yourselves, and I've been honored to work with you.

Special thanks to members of my Real World Prepping group on Facebook for your input on various topics we've discussed that eventually found their way into this book.

Any writer is only as good as his editors, so I'd like to thank the team at Ulysses Press for all their hard work and dedication to making this book as great as it can be.

Last but not least, I have to thank Ben Harris, Sebastian Raatz, Annabel Vered, Skye Back, and the rest of the team at Centennial Media. Manning the helm for *Prepper Survival Guide* and *Backwoods Survival Guide* magazines has been absolutely a dream job and I look forward to working with all of you for years to come.

ABOUT THE AUTHOR

Jim Cobb is a recognized authority on disaster readiness and related topics. He is the editor-in-chief of *Prepper Survival Guide* and *Backwoods Survival Guide* magazines. He's authored more than ten books, including *Prepper's Home Defense* and *The Prepper's Complete Book of Disaster Readiness*. Jim has been involved with emergency preparedness in one capacity or another for almost four decades. He and his wife have three sons and a houseful of assorted critters. You can find Jim online on Facebook (facebook.com/jim.cobb.739/) or email him directly: jim@survivalweekly.com.